"Llego a preguntarme a veces si las formas superiores de la emoción estética no consistirán, simplemente, en un supremo entendimiento de lo creado … un día se sabrá que cada caracol era, desde siempre, un poema."

Alejo Carpentier in *"Los pasos perdidos"*, 1953

GEOMETRIC TAXONOMY

CARLOS FERRATER & OAB

IGNACIO PARICIO

INDEX

1. A TAXONOMY OF GEOMETRIC MANIPULATIONS 09

I. Simple shapes
Torroella, "El Terrat" Studios, Roca Gallery, Villa-real 11
City Hall Palma, Hospitalet, Toulouse, C.N.Estartit 13
Children's Holiday Center, Regina House 15

II. Combinations of simple shapes
A. Juxtapositions
Impiva, Alonso House, Library at Bellaterra 17
Convention Center, Evangelical Church, Fisersa 19
Tagomago Villa 21
Nolla House, F3 House, Andorra Casino 23
B. Intersections
Fort Pienc, CSIC, Municipal housing 25
MediaPro Building 27
Hippodrome Tower, Artabria Archaeological Museum 29

III. Voids in simple shapes
A. Central voids
Fitness Center, BF House 31
House for a Photographer II 33
Triginer House, Molinet House, Kaplankaya, Almaty 35
B. Peripheral voids
Binisafúa House, House-Studio in Llampaies 37
Buildings in Passeig de Gràcia, Ria Bilbao 39
Blocks on Poblenou, Houses on Carrer Fernando Poo 41

IV. Breaking down surfaces into discrete elements
A. Irregular elements
Botanic Garden 43
Science Museum and Park in Granada 45
Azahar, Urban Planning for Garellano, Six Senses Hotel 47
B. Geometric elements
Zaragoza Station, Frontaura Winery, Edition Hotel 49
Housing in Plaça de Lesseps, Vértix Housing 51
AA House 53

V. Displacement of lines to form a generatrix
Housing on the chamfer in Passeig de Gràcia 55
Hall Hotel Juan Carlos I, IMQ Zorrotzaure, tower in the 22@ 57
Museum in Lyon, Benidorm Seafront 59
Table of taxonomies 61

2. GEOMETRY IN THE DESIGN PROCESS 63

I. Geometry as a provocative suggestion
Oteiza's chalk models and Impiva 65
Picasso and the house at Alcanar 67
Joanet's pieces of cardboard and the Museum in Lyon 69

II. Geometry to guarantee accuracy
AA House: the painful process of achieving accuracy 71
MediaPro Building: a homogeneous grid 73
Isotropic corners 75

III. Geometry as a design tool
Triginer House: the "chop" 77
Botanic Garden: a ductile grid 79
Benidorm: tactile continuity 81

3. GEOMETRY AND COMPOSITION

I. The disappearance of composition as a discipline 83

II. Style versus syntax 85

III. Geometry as OAB's shared language 87

LIST OF CREDITS FOR DESIGNS AND WORKS APPEARING IN THE PUBLICATION 88

BIBLIOGRAPHICAL NOTES 94

The abscense of scale
The idea of scale may be unconsistent under certain conditions. Reaching the feeling of having no need of measuring, allows you to catch a glimpse of a limit place; a place where it is posible to experience at the real size the project and the construction.
Carlos Ferrater
OAB
OAB
OAB
OAB

FOREWORD

I got into this all on my own.

My relationship with this subject began more than 20 years ago during a visit to Carlos Ferrater's studio, when I was lucky enough to see his design for the Botanic Garden in Barcelona. I was interested in his explanation of the design process. He had superimposed a geometric grid on the site and distorted some of its elements as a way of approaching the design process.

Sometime later, Ferrater was the winning candidate in a competitive process to choose a new architecture tenure chair, and I was on the jury. His presentation, like others I had heard him give, revolved around discussing specific projects, but the works themselves were much more powerful than his line of argument.

I suggested to him that he should introduce his use of geometry as a way to explain his work. I don't know if my insistence had anything to do with *Synchronizing Geometry*, the book he and his son Borja published in 2006.

Almost 15 years later, when I saw the magnificent Absence of Scale exhibition online, my attention was drawn to the regularity and repetition of his geometric manipulations.

Perhaps his insistence on the expression "absence of scale" owes to the fact that scaling buildings down and making all his models small enough to be produced on a 3D printer emphasizes their volume and encourages an abstract geometrical approach.

His approach reminded me once more of my conviction that geometry is a thread that runs through all of Ferrater's works and made me think it might be possible to create a taxonomy of his formal strategies. I immediately began studying his work to find out more about the relationship between these projects and geometry.

And that's how I got myself into this.

Exhibition "The absence of scale" at the OAB Gallery

1. TAXONOMY OF GEOMETRIC MANIPULATIONS

Geometry is present in all architectural buildings. Whatever their shape, they are defined by some kind of mathematical instrument, even if this consists of no more than a series of points in space, which is sometimes the case in provocatively formless kinds of architecture. We have no choice but to accept that there is geometry to all architectural forms, however random they may seem.

In this book, however, I focus on something else. I examine the geometries present in timeless architecture: the architecture described in detail in the great treatises, the architecture that dazzles us with what Le Corbusier described as "a learned game, correct and magnificent, of forms assembled in the light," the elementary shapes that inspired Modern architecture a century ago.

All architects are forced to design and define their works in geometrical terms, and this science forms part—or should form part—of their professional experience. But in some architects' designs, geometry plays a much more important role. Geometry can be used to suggest new shapes, to make designs strictly accurate, and even as a design tool. I will examine these three aspects at the end of the book, which is organized as follows: in the first section, I attempt to create a taxonomy of the different forms of geometrical manipulation; in the second, I examine how geometry is introduced into the design process; and in the third, I analyze the relationships between composition and geometry over the course of Carlos Ferrater's career and OAB's work.

In the first section, I use the following taxonomical groups to classify the different designs:

I. **SIMPLE SHAPES**

II. **REDUCTION TO ELEMENTARY GEOMETRY**
- **A. JUXTAPOSITIONS**
- **B. INTERSECTIONS**

III. **VOIDS IN ELEMENTARY SHAPES**
- **A. CENTRAL VOIDS**
- **B. PERIPHERAL VOIDS**

IV. **BREAKING DOWN SURFACES INTO DISCRETE ELEMENTS**
- **A. IRREGULAR ELEMENTS**
- **B. GEOMETRIC ELEMENTS**

V. **DISPLACEMENT OF LINES TO FORM A GENERATRIX**

First cardboard model of the hall of the Hotel Juan Carlos

I. SIMPLE SHAPES

Pure prisms are a frequent choice in the formal minimalism that became the lingua franca of architecture in the second half of the 20th century. Throughout his career, Carlos Ferrater has often used these simple volumes.

His preference for elementary geometries became evident very early on, appearing in 1982 when work began on the **TORROELLA DE MONTGRÍ SPORTS CENTER** project. The hall is virtually a pure glass prism and is a direct response to a simple brief. As I will explore later, this volumetric simplicity is not automatic. It is the result of certain structural artifices that enabled the construction of a magnificent, transparent, entirely isotropic prism and a two-way prismatic image, based on a frame structure that is directional and thus anisotropic. I will return to this theme in chapter 2.II.c.

Some years later, with **EL TERRAT FILM STUDIOS** (Barcelona, 1995–97), Ferrater once again drew a perfect low box with an enormous opening in the facade, which he used to make life inside the film studio visible.

He has continued to use this approach throughout his professional life, at least until he designed the spectacular prism of thick, laminated glass that forms the exhibition hall at the **ROCA GALLERY** in Barcelona, which he designed in partnership with his son, Borja, and daughter, Lucía, in 2009. Here the prism forms an innovative envelope made of packages of laminated glass, the appearance of which is spectacular due to its transparency and the refraction of light inside it.

But in other cases, this minimalism is the result of an effort to fit a complex brief into an elementary shape, as at the **VILA-REAL LIBRARY** (2009–11). A screen of ceramic bars, a tribute to the local tile industry, surrounds the whole building. Between this continuous envelope and the varied, slightly set back, internal facade, a rich intermediate space is formed.

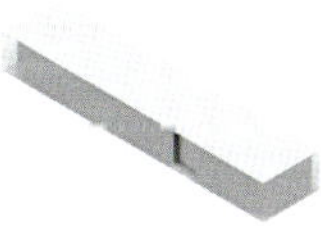

In other designs, Carlos Ferrater repeats the idea of juxtaposing elementary shapes on entirely different scales. He has frequently used large vertical blocks, as in the design for **PALMA DE MALLORCA CITY HALL** (2007), where four square towers are arranged in an orderly military parade.

The **SOCIAL HOUSING DEVELOPMENT IN L'HOSPITALET** (2012–14) is the most recent work in which he plays with the orderly proximity of three towers, this time rectangular ones, giving the whole design an impressive solidity. The simple shape of the blocks is common to all these designs, but their relative organization is not. This leads us to the later chapter on juxtaposition (1.II.A).

53 SOCIAL HOUSING, ZAC ANDROMÈDE IN TOULOUSE (2013–16) dates from around the same time and, like Ferrater's other projects in France, was designed in partnership with Alberto Peñín. Here, he once again uses the same resource, combining the ordered vertical prisms of the towers with the oblong horizontal body of the base. The interaction between simple shapes became increasingly important in his work and began to approach the grouped juxtapositions discussed in the next section.

Ferrater also uses few simple shapes that are not parallelepipeds. The most important and oldest of these projects is **L'ESTARTIT SAILING CLUB** (1988–91), in which the massive sloping roof creates a flattened pyramid shape, like a ship whose prow is entering the port. The shape of the whole building is actually much more complex, but the almost triangular facade overlooking the sea is what creates this image. It is a very flat pyramid with a strong vertical line between the vertex and one of the corners of the base.

The most curious and appealing design using these elementary shapes produced small constructions shaped like a child's typical drawing of a house for the **CHILDREN'S HOLIDAY CENTER AT VILADOMS** (2010). The purity of the cubic prisms, topped by pyramids, is an abstraction that is a far cry from the requirements of traditional construction, which is always so picturesque. There are no projections or eaves or hipped roofs sticking out anywhere. Achieving such simplicity of form required considerable design effort in construction terms.

In fact, the true construction is wrapped in an external wall insulation system (EWIS) that Ferrater had already tried out at the Azahar offices. This enabled the plaster protecting the insulation to be applied continuously to the corners and edges of the roof. The company that installed the system was rather unsure about its use on roofs, which had not been tried before, but in the end they agreed, and the success of the idea can be seen here. The construction system is not only economical, it also lends itself to the production of these simple, abstract shapes. The grouping of "little houses" of different sizes is also associated with the idea of the juxtaposition of simple shapes.

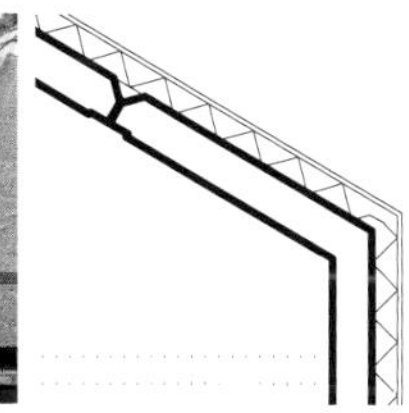

I also want to include a very recent construction in this section—the **REGINA HOUSE** (Gaüses, 2019). The prisms topped by sloping forms have evolved from more elementary shapes. The roofs of the two sections of the building are reminiscent of the houses at the holiday center but slope inwards, forming an impluvium.

C

II. COMBINATIONS OF SIMPLE SHAPES

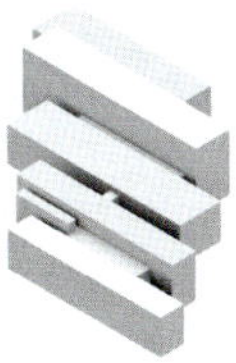

A. JUXTAPOSITIONS

I have already discussed some examples of simple shapes built close together, but the formal interaction between these was limited to their orderly arrangement. The most interesting juxtaposition is the **IMPIVA TECHNOLOGY PARK** (Castelló de la Plana, 1993–95). This is a set of prisms in the form of narrow vertical blocks that are arranged parallel to one another and close together, such that they create a facade or front for the whole building. The facades alternate warm materials like Prodema with cold ones such as Alucobond. The different materials and proportions bring the building to life, as does the parallel layout of the blocks.

It is an ingenious design based on a functional organization that attempts to meet diverse objectives. The result is a segmented building that creates an entirely new language for this type of construction. As the project report says, "it is a system, a set of autonomous boxes, which come together to form a more complex, higher-order microorganism." A successful venture into the language of juxtapositions.

The success of Ferrater's experiment in form at Impiva made its mark on subsequent designs in which he also juxtaposed vertical volumes, such as the **ALONSO PLANAS HOUSE**. (Esplugues, 1995–98). Large-scale lattices of horizontal concrete strips were also used in another contemporary composition of juxtapositions: the Catalonia Convention Center in Barcelona.

He revisited the grouping of vertical boxes used at the Impiva Technology Park in an unbuilt design he entered in the competition for the **UNIVERSITY LIBRARY AT BELLATERRA** (1998), although the form was more closely packed and vertical.

The **CATALONIA CONVENTION CENTER** (1996–2000) can also be read as a juxtaposition of volumes, although it is more difficult to take in visually. The functional requirements of the various parts of the building make them harder to recognize as simple prisms. Some roofs were raised to accommodate the larger halls, but for the passer-by, the building looks exactly like series of juxtaposed blocks, as the picture here shows. This succession of prisms is highlighted by the presence of the large lattices of horizontal concrete strips. These were used in other designs from this period discussed above.

The series is made up of two large, low sections containing the largest halls. A third vertical contains the facade, in a similar fashion to the Impiva blocks, and then there is a final curved block that emphasizes the triangular shape of the site.

Whenever the brief has allowed, Ferrater has returned to simple shapes. The most recent example of this is the **EVANGELICAL CHURCH** (Terrassa, 2008–10), where two boxes were arranged alongside each other on a huge plinth. The two volumes are perfect prisms covered with aluminum honeycomb panels. A wide-angle view of the corners underlines the perfect isotropy.

This juxtaposition of elementary volumes is a handy resource that OAB has used in quite a few other works. One curious example because it is something of a mixture is the **FISERSA HEADQUARTERS** (Figueres 1998). This consists of a set of prismatic volumes that seem to form part of a larger whole, a combination of juxtaposition, intersection, and voids, like the works I discuss later on.

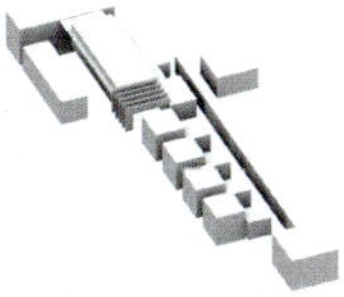

The **TAGOMAGO VILLA** (Ibiza, 1999–2000) is an interesting design that could be considered the paradigm of juxtaposed elementary volumes because of the strength that comes from arraying identical parts of the building in a line.

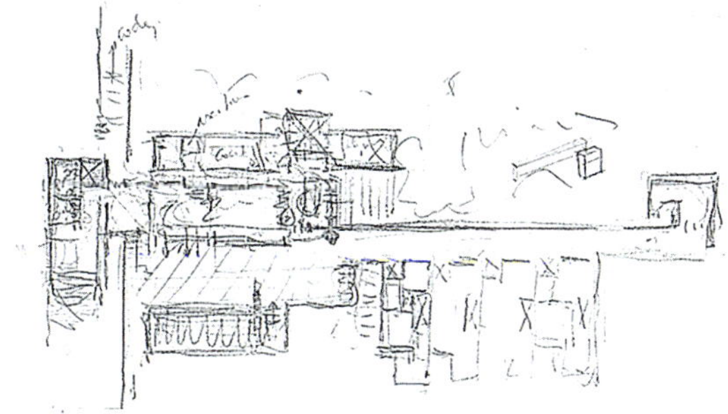

"The project evolved like a typical rural construction, by adding different sections and rooms, placing great importance on the spatial and environmental routes between these white sandstone volumes standing in the bright Mediterranean sun. This achieves an atmosphere that recalls both Arab and southern Mediterranean architecture while at the same time providing a relaxed, serene finish, almost like a monastic building. This is furthered by the use of two pure, unmanipulated materials—sandstone and white concrete that was poured on-site.

"This organization, consisting of independent, isolated sections, makes it possible to create a series of open spaces, courtyards, porches, and terraces, blurring the boundaries between the indoors and the outdoors."

The volumetrics of the building derived from the brief, which came from a three-generation extended family. Relatively independent accommodation for each group is resolved in a highly democratic way: all the "houses" that make up the villa are the same. The building is a drawn-out series of boxes arrayed along a central axis. Its location on the site is discreet, almost hidden from the sea. This line of boxes stretches across the site until it reaches the final building—the parents' house. This overlooks a cliff with the sea as a backdrop. The best location for this pavilion-style design on the site was chosen carefully.

In the designs described so far, the use of juxtaposition has been horizontal, using more or less vertical boxes arranged one beside another. At the **NOLLA HOUSE** (Esplugues, 2004–08), OAB tried out a new model: a vertical juxtaposition of flat boxes displaced and piled on top of one another. The apparent simplicity of the piled-up boxes was extremely laborious in construction terms. Although each floor slab is the ceiling for the story below it in the normal way, the upper box extends out over the lower one. For it to appear as though one form were literally resting on the other, each slab needed to fold up and out so that the overhanging section is higher than the rest. These folds in the slabs created vertical beams which enabled the ribs of the building to be arranged differently, spanning large areas. Only by designing the slabs this way could the corners of the prisms be cleanly separated.

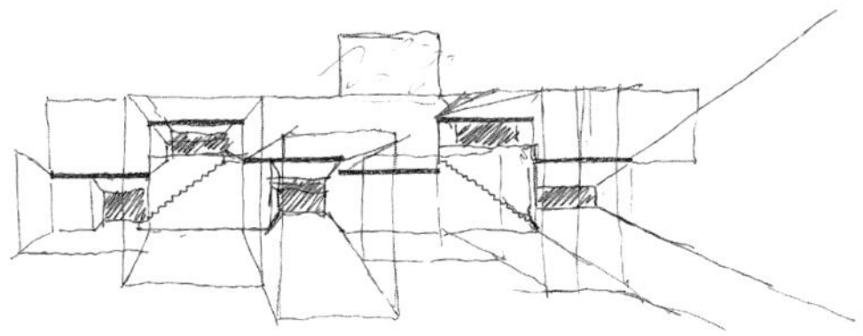

The **F3 HOUSE** in Barcelona (2007–09) shows another way of piling up almost cubic shapes that was even harder to achieve. Here the juxtaposition is both vertical and horizontal, with overhangs and offsetting to make terraces, corners, and quiet porches. The aligned repetition of elevated cubes is reminiscent of the successful juxtaposition at Tagomago.

At the **ANDORRA CASINO** (2017), the building is also a pile of slightly offset volumes, although here the front of each slab sometimes forms part of the floor above it and sometimes of the one below. This prevents changes in floor levels in the projection.

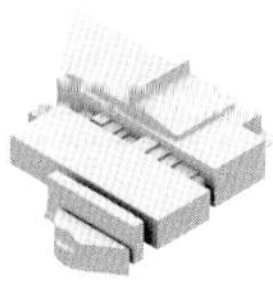

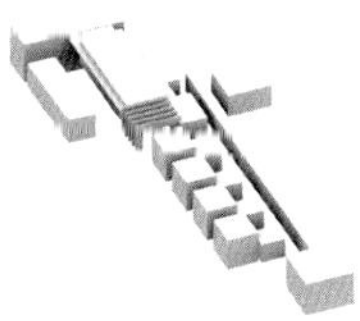

II. COMBINATIONS OF SIMPLE SHAPES

B. INTERSECTIONS

The next group is the taxonomy is intersections: buildings with simple volumes that cut through one another. The first of these are two older projects that could be called classics and use similar forms of interpenetration. The first is the **FORT PIENC SOCIAL SERVICES CENTER IN BARCELONA**, designed in partnership with Lucía Ferrater (2001–03), in which a series of prisms fit into one another like drawers on a telescopic guide rail. One section appears to contain the other: there could hardly be a more radical form of intersection. The different materials enveloping each box—aluminum latticework, exposed concrete, and glass—help to radically differentiate the sections.

The **CSIC** (Higher Council of Scientific Research) building in the Barcelona Botanic Gardens was constructed at the same time (2001–02) and belongs to the same family of intersections, in that one of the volumes appears to envelop the other entirely. The picture here shows it as a solid white block encircling an eye-catching darker section with plenty of glass. Here, as at Fort Pienc, the fact that the two sections are separate is made clearer through the use of different materials. The volumes can be interpreted in various ways because the white section with the stainless steel and wooden prism embedded in it actually has a lower counterweight, and the wooden prism hangs from large beams at the top.

Shortly afterward, in a **DEVELOPMENT FOR THE MUNICIPAL HOUSING COMPANY** (2002–05) in the Villaverde district of southern Madrid, he tried out a stepped layout that begins to suggest intersecting vertical forms—a forerunner of successful later projects.

The most sculptural volume is the **MEDIAPRO BUILDING** in Avinguda Diagonal (Barcelona, 2005–08). This consists of an intersection of prismatic volumes that respond to how the diagonal avenue breaks the grid pattern of the streets in the area of the city designed by Cerdà in the late 19th century. Ferrater's determination to use two intersecting shapes that respected the layout of the surrounding streets is clear from the very first sketch. The vertical lines form part of the geometry of this part of the city, while the slanting lines are respectfully perpendicular to those of Avinguda Diagonal.

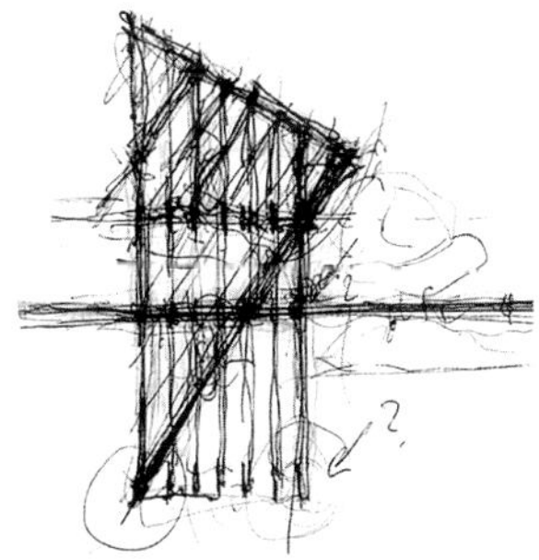

"The facade of the building turns to run respectfully parallel to the Diagonal, Barcelona's most iconic avenue. There is an opening in the first four floors of the building to allow the last block of Carrer Bolívia to pass through it, creating a focus point... The base of the tower starts below the top of this opening, on the same level as the plinth of the neighboring building, and is offset, creating a new plane, forming the facade that runs along Avinguda Diagonal, and opening up views of the neighboring building. The top floors of the main building run toward the edge of the tower on the diagonal, the geometry of which gives a sculptural finish. The interaction between these two layouts creates a dynamic interplay of shadows. The lower body or plinth penetrates the other section below the tower and its transparent facade creates a new kind of public space: a triangular city square. Ranged around it, the building is a respectful sculpture that responds to the city's needs."

After completing the MediaPro Building, the architect presented a design for the **HEADQUARTERS OF THE CATALAN LAND AGENCY INCASOL** in Barcelona (2008), the layout of which again used intersecting forms that respected their surroundings. It would have been a magnificent building, perhaps even more ambitious than the previous one.

The **HIPPODROME TOWER** (Guadalajara, 2012–18), an office block in Mexico, appears to be a similar type of intersection to the MediaPro building, but in fact it is rather more complex. It is a large, faceted, staggered volume interpreted differently depending on the viewpoint. Seen from its most spectacular side, it appears to be a Flatiron-like shape intersecting with a smaller lateral block. Seen from the opposite side, it looks like a set of intersecting, terraced forms.

On the main facade, the forcefulness of this interpenetration is reinforced by the strict continuity of the envelope. According to the architects, this concrete lattice is a nod to Barragán and suggests a more locally inspired approach than a cold, American-influenced office block. However, when lit up from within at night, the building fits with the iconography of the International Style.

I would like to end this chapter on intersections with a fascinating design that was never built, the **ARTABRIA ARCHAEOLOGICAL MUSEUM** (A Coruña, 2003), which used a very different type of intersection.

"The building is a large frame structure embedded in the northern slope of the town of Mesoiro. The section that is most deeply embedded in the hill is intended for the museum galleries while the projecting part is for other facilities... The building is laid out as five large containers with uniform geometries (repeated lengths of 17 m and 20 m), generating a 375-meter zig-zag route through the museum."

To achieve this zig-zag without interrupting the route, the containers intersect at some of their ends. The way the design adapts to the topography of the site enriches the volumetrics of this set of interlinked prisms.

III. VOIDS IN SIMPLE SHAPES

A. CENTRAL VOIDS

I now turn to a completely different approach, one that involves altering the volume of simple parts of buildings using different kinds of voids. Although this may be a rather arbitrary exercise, I will distinguish central voids from peripheral ones. I define voids as central if part of the volume is removed to create a space that is surrounded by the functional activity of the building. This is more important than the exact location of the void vis-à-vis the geometric volume.

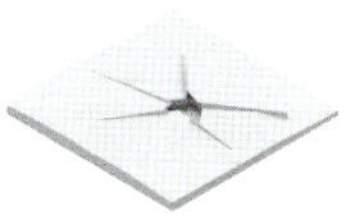

These central voids result in the most radical designs. According to Ferrater, this is where all problems converge. The **FITNESS CENTER** (Barcelona, 1993–96) at the Juan Carlos Hotel is an imposing example of this type of void, because a volume was literally extracted from below ground. The built section is sunk below ground level and the central star-shaped opening appears surprisingly below the lawn, forming a central courtyard which all the areas of the gym look onto.

Perhaps the building where the use of this strategy is most radical is the **BF HOUSE** (Castelló, 2006–11), where the central square was extracted from the single volume of the oblong prism. The result is spectacular: as part of the house projects out over a slope, this opening can also be seen and experienced from below. The strategy also made it possible to leave the site and its vegetation virtually intact.

In **HOUSE FOR A PHOTOGRAPHER II** (Alcanar, 2005–06), a detached house Ferrater designed for his brother, the central void is not the result of an extraction but is instead the gap between small built volumes. The proximity of these sections creates both this void and some intermediate spaces. The richness of the intermediate spaces is surprising, as they bring views of the neighboring market and the sea.

"*The central void thereby becomes the main space in the house, a taut area that is delineated geometrically at the top by the high, opaque forms of the different blocks.*"

This design might also fit into the juxtaposition category. Indeed, the building's ultimate layout looks more like spaces between blocks than a void in a single original block. But we have placed it here because it is a magnificent example of how a central void can form the nucleus for the whole brief. The spaces between the sections of the designs included in the chapter on juxtapositions are generally residual rather than central.

The three blocks receive light from this central space and are accessed through it, bringing it to life and making it the hub of activity in the house. The pictures here show how similar the central voids of the Fitness Center and the house at Alcanar ultimately are to one another when seen from the sections surrounding them. In the Fitness Center, the visual relationship between the different interior spaces via the courtyard is identical to that of the house at Alcanar, although in the former it is merely a means for light to reach the underground interiors.

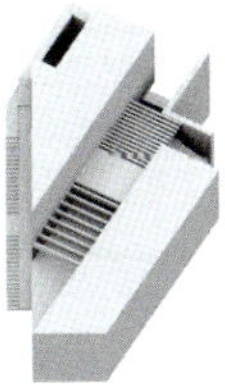

The **TRIGINER HOUSE** (1993–96) is an interesting example because of the leading role that geometry played in the design process, as I will explore later. For now, I will simply note that it is another case in which the void might be classified either as peripheral or central. There is no doubt, however, that it is the center of activity in the house; the feature that resolves all the functional connections—"the wheelhouse," as the owner would have it.

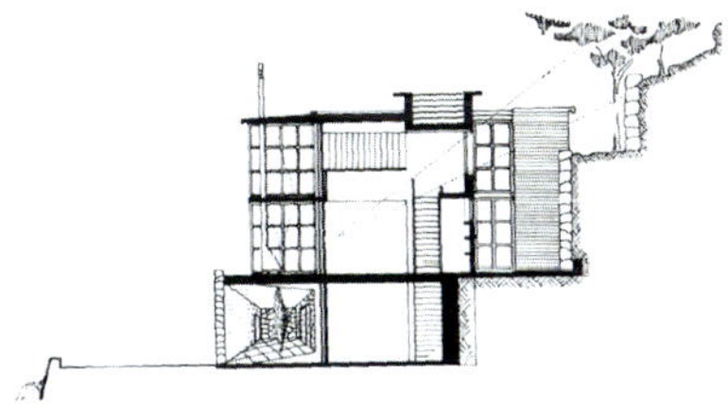

There are other projects in which Ferrater uses spectacular central voids to organize the forms and functions of the building, but in which these are not entirely open to the outside. Perhaps the oldest of these is the **MOLINET HOUSE** (L'Estartit, 1996–98).

"The design was approached from the section. A large central void acts as a dual space, with views of the mountains (via a large arched window overlooking the rear courtyard) and the sea (through the large window shaped like a ship's prow)."

Another design with a hidden central courtyard is the **KAPLANKAYA CLUBHOUSE**, (Bodrum, Turkish coast, 2011–13). In this case, the internal void forms the cloister/foyer of the club, but it is largely covered. The central courtyard is visible from the outside through large skylights, which allow us to classify the space as a void in the compact building.

The design for the **MODERN ART MUSEUM IN ALMATY** (Kazakhstan, 2016) is similar. Here a huge cylindrical central space is surrounded by windowless towers whose exterior perimeter almost entirely follows the line of a square prism. The central space is merely hinted at in the aerial view because the roof of the large opening is slightly below the line of the roof. The slashes between these towers form perimetral voids bringing light into the central space. Voids of this type are the focus of the next chapter.

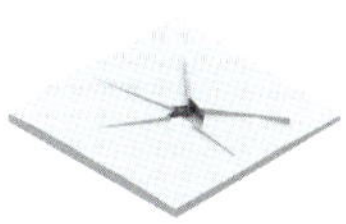

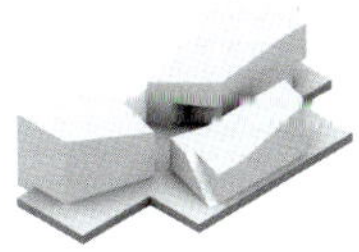

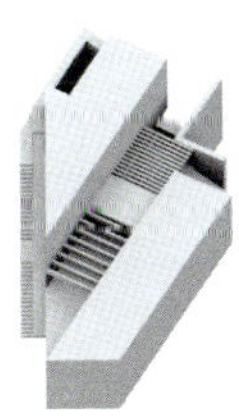

III. VOIDS IN SIMPLE SHAPES

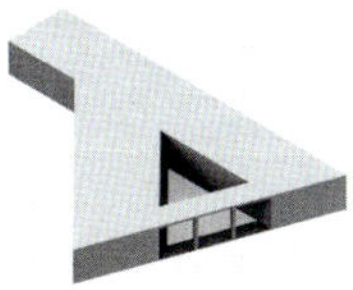

B. PERIPHERAL VOIDS

The **BINISAFÚA HOUSE** (Menorca, 1988–90) is an example of the transition between the two kinds of voids. Its courtyard could be classified as either central or peripheral, and it could even be described as the intersection of two prismatic volumes opening onto the sea to form a Y shape. But I prefer to read it as a peripheral void in an almost triangular volume on to which the most important rooms in the house open, overlooking the Menorcan sea via a portico.

The **HOUSE-STUDIO IN LLAMPAIES** (1992–93) is the first Carlos built for his photographer brother, before the house at Alcanar. Like the latter, this house consists of several "monofunctional," highly differentiated sections around a central feature. But in this case, the feature is a hall rather than a void, and the voids in the design are peripheral, although their function is almost exclusively to separate the different sections from each other almost entirely. The volumetric design is rather similar to the second house, but this is a centrifugal design, looking outwards, while the other is centripetal, looking inward. Views of the countryside and the sea only creep in through the cracks. Describing Alcanar, Carlos writes:

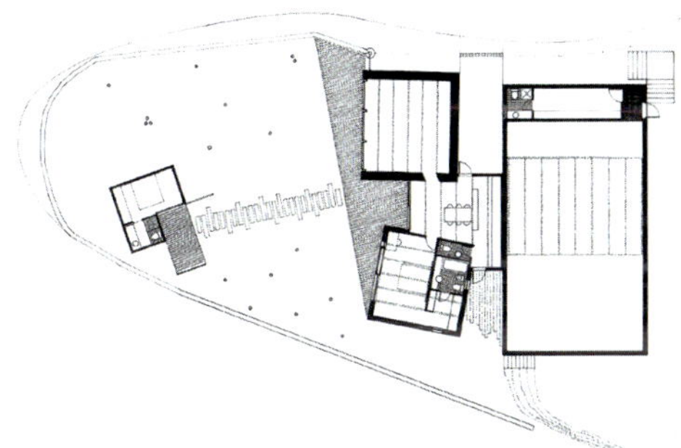

"in short, it was the same plan as at Llampaies, but whereas the climate at the latter meant that the connecting space was a room that was an allegory of the hall joining all the rooms in traditional Catalan farmhouses, the climate at Alcanar mean that the same space—this time open to the elements—would function as the spatial hub for the project, in the spirit of the old farmhouses and constructions of the southern Mediterranean." [1]

The Banco Comercial Trasatlántico building has stood on one of the most iconic sites in Barcelona for 50 years. The building was designed by Santiago Balcells, the winner of a competition in the 1960s. A tower set perpendicularly to the street stood on a lower section, the awkward geometry of which was required to adapt the building to its location between Avinguda Diagonal, Passeig de Gràcia, and the square formed between them.

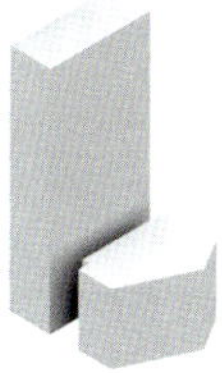

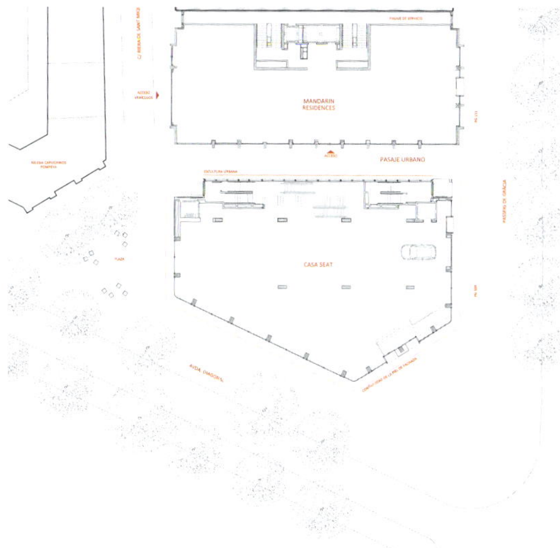

The commission received for the **BUILDING AT THE INTERSECTION OF AVDA. DIAGONAL AND PASSEIG DE GRÀCIA** (2017–21) required combining two entirely different briefs: luxury housing and a showroom bringing car manufacturer SEAT into the center of Barcelona. Ferrater's approach was radical. A deep cut took the volume of the tower down toward the ground, separating it from the rest of the low building used as the car showroom. The resulting passageway is not central from a functional point of view, as it is lined by blocks with very different functions, making it an extremely radical, effective geometric intervention.

Peripheral voids are not usually so imposing. Once they have investigated and assimilated an approach that involves “cutting into” their designs, architects can use incisions, tears, and other surface voids with a lighter hand than in designs where they are mainly used to create a particular image when seen from the outside. One example of this is the **2 APARTMENT BUILDINGS IN BILBAO** (2008–11), in which the voids serve to break down the large construction block into sections.

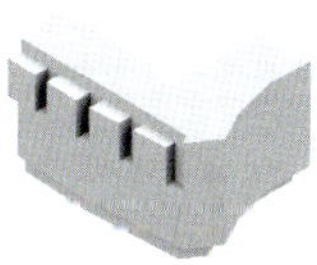

The design for **FIVE BLOCKS ON POBLENOU SEAFRONT** (1989–92) was based on Cerdà's vision of the city block as rings of housing ranged around a central courtyard or space. However, aligned breaks in the three blocks connect the spaces at the center of each via a lane or passageway.

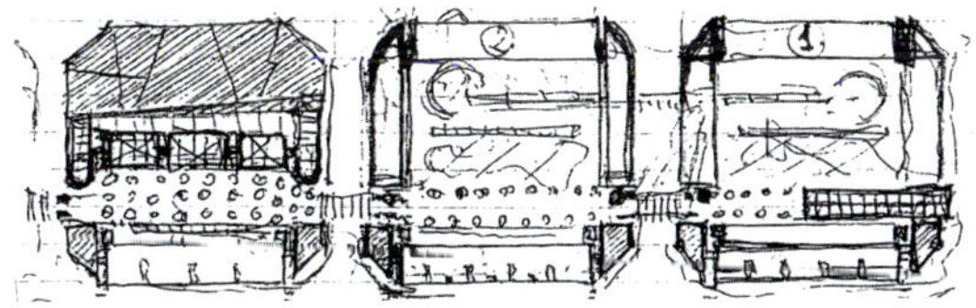

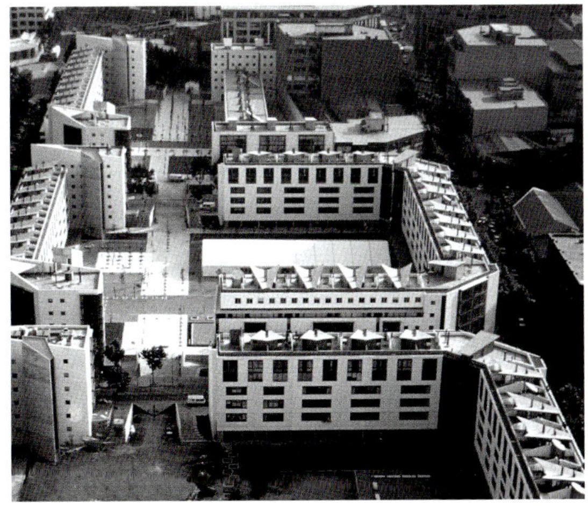

These passageways are reminiscent of those in Cerdà's design for Barcelona, which crossed through the center of each city block. However, the gardens Ferrater included for leisure and recreation are absolutely in line with more modern attempts to design friendly, inclusive public spaces.

The initial sketches show how the architect suffered when it came to the chamfers at the corners. These are one of Cerdà's great contributions to architecture but incorporating them into right-angled geometry is extremely hard. At the chamfers on Carrer Llull, at the top of the sketch, the lines seem to insist on creating a fissure between the part of the building that runs along the street and the chamfer. At the other end of the complex, looking onto Carrer Ramón Turró, the sections on the chamfer are separated radically from the rest of the building and a break once again solves the problem, creating a narrow passageway between the street and the inner space. Two different approaches to creating incisions in buildings have become the guiding force behind the design.

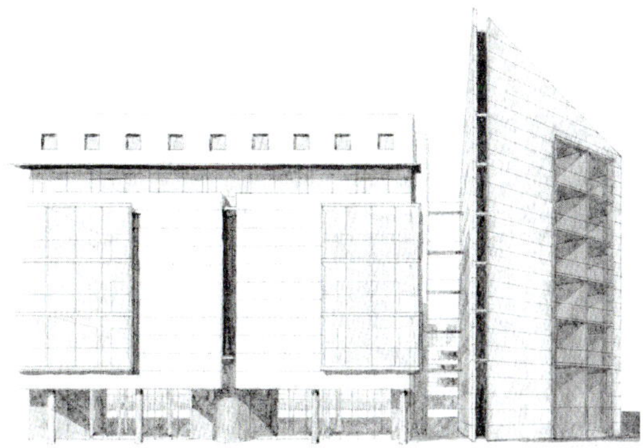

I will end this exploration of examples of peripheral spaces with the **TWELVE HOUSES ON CARRER FERNANDO POO** (Barcelona, 2016–18), one of Carlos Ferrater's more recent works. The breaks in the facade chop it up, bringing light into the rooms at the back, while creating a rhythm of cubic shapes that is reminiscent of the Iagomago House.

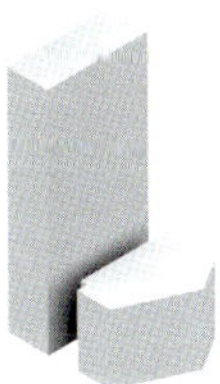

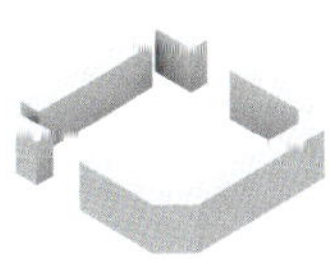

IV. BREAKING DOWN SURFACES INTO DISCRETE ELEMENTS

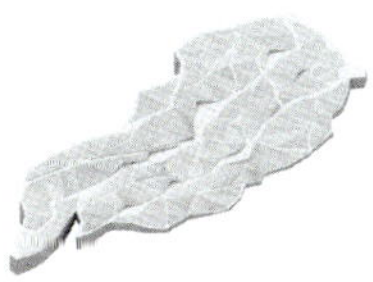

A. IRREGULAR ELEMENTS

The geometrical manipulations that I focus on in this section are very unlike those described above. They are highly original and can no longer be conceived of as classical compositional manipulations.

In general, they involve deforming or distorting a surface by virtually or actually breaking it down into a grid that acts as the guide for subsequent geometrical transformations. Ferrater's earliest attempt at this was the **BOTANIC GARDEN** (Barcelona 1995–99), which became a model for his subsequent projects and clearly illustrates how useful geometrical manipulation can be in the design process.

Later in the book I will look at the design process that led to the solution that was eventually built, but here I would like to highlight how important this project has been in Ferrater's career. Breaking a surface down into discrete elements to form a giant grid has become a fundamental design tool for the studio. Applying it to the roofs of large buildings led to the idea of treating those roofs as artificial topographies.

In the case of the Botanic Garden, the grid was used over the entire site, first adapting to it, then being used to lay out paths, facilities, and the beds for each planting block. By manipulating the triangles that the grid was made up of, banks were raised, and routes and platforms created. The initial view of the park, top right, was eventually submerged beneath the vegetation which naturally took on the shape of the design grid.

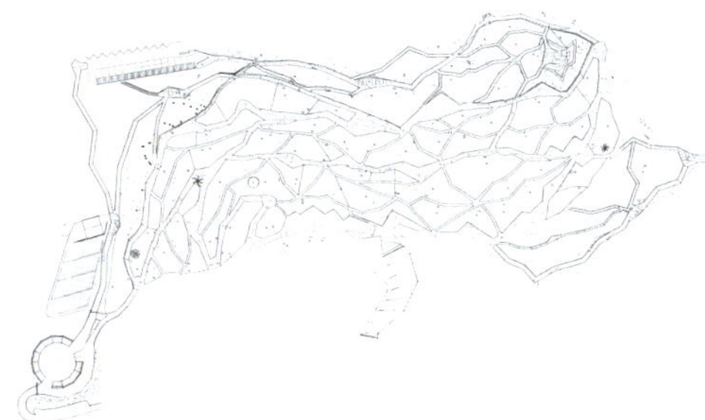

CLINICA INMACULADA

At the **SCIENCE MUSEUM AND PARK IN GRANADA** (2004–08), which was built a few years after the Botanic Garden, this idea of breaking down a surface into irregular, discrete elements became the guiding force behind the design.

In this project, rather than using a relatively continuous grid made up of similar components, Ferrater superimposed a polygonal grid on to the floorplan of the building and then manipulated it.

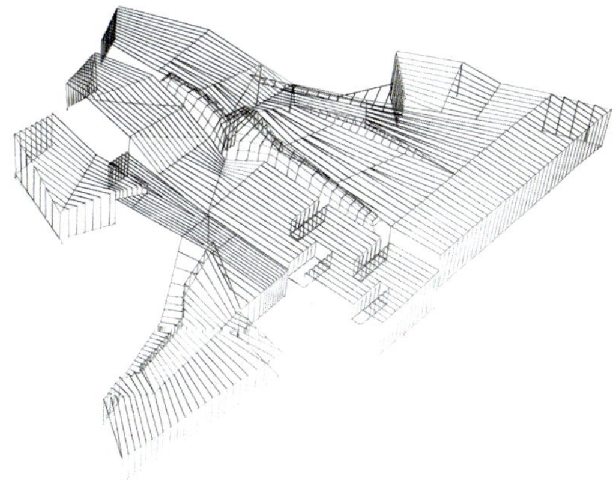

In his words:

"We architects have always been obsessed with creating buildings that construct topography. However, I believe there are few truly topographical buildings. The Yokohama sea terminal, which could be one, is, in fact, a succession of porticoes, like the ribs of a boat molded in the shape of a honeycomb. But it isn't a topography—there is a final portico.[2] I had always imagined creating a design by rolling out a topography. In Granada, the floor and the roof run over broken terrain, adapting to the different points connecting the site with the city, the River Genil, and the existing buildings. The roof, which has been freed from slavish attachment to the ground, creates a sense of spaciousness.[3] The spectacular internal spaces are housed between the two topographies—the ground and the roof."

The photograph here seeks to show the parallels between the Sierra Nevada mountains in the distance and the topographical shape of the roof, which is made up of a grid of irregular, manipulated components.

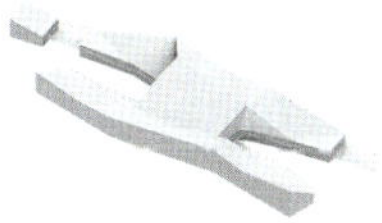

This strategy was repeated three years later in the design for the **AZAHAR GROUP HEADQUARTERS** (Castelló de la Plana, 2007–08). The way the folded polygonal grid competes with the surrounded topography is even clearer, and the bulky, rounded shapes of the nearby hills are reproduced in the folds of the roof. With the exception of the central skylights, the entire roof is resolved using an external insulation system like that of the Children's Holiday Center at Viladoms. The aerial photo clearly shows how the relatively simple parallel sections of the building are roofed with a plane made up of subtle components, its vertices pulled upward or downward to form a topographical roof whose gray facets stand out among the orange trees that surround the building.

Almost contemporary with this roof was the design presented for the **URBAN PLANNING FOR GARELLANO** (Bilbao, 2009) competition. Once again, OAB used large-scaled folds in the roof design, this time slightly more forced as the blocks were quite high.

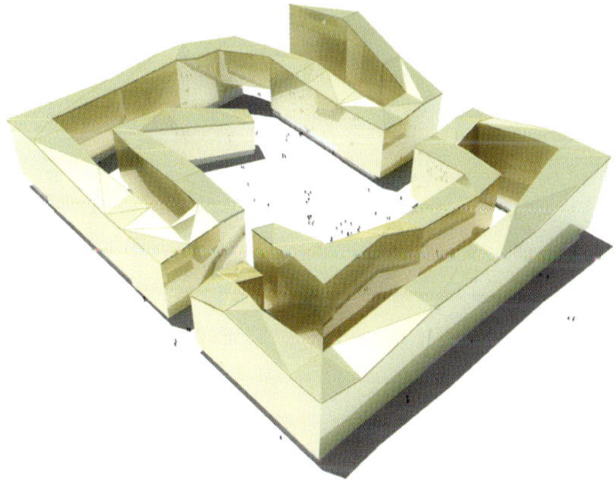

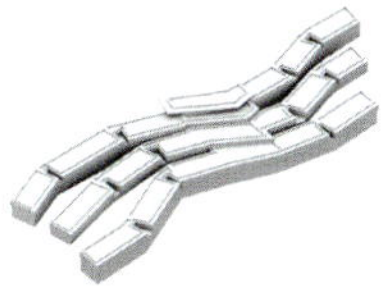

The **KAPLANKAYA SIX SENSES WELLNESS RESORT** (Bodrum, 2012–16) is related to these strategies. On this site, the whole building, not just the roof, is once again broken down into discrete elements that are articulated with one another over different levels, imitating traditional Mediterranean farming terraces. The central section, which is also the largest, contains the hotel's public spaces and serves as a nexus between the different levels the interconnected sections of the building are arrayed across.

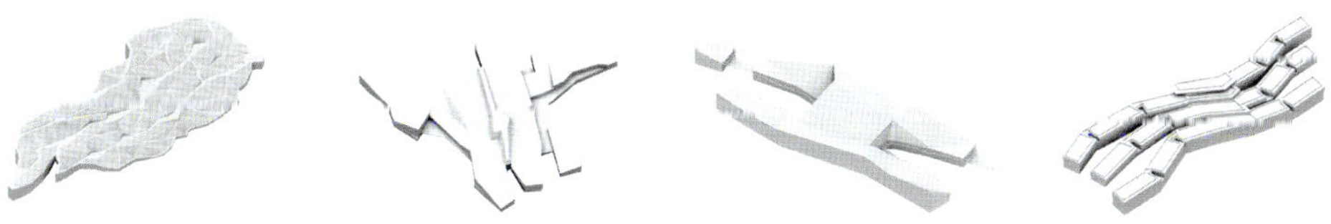

IV. BREAKING DOWN SURFACES INTO DISCRETE ELEMENTS

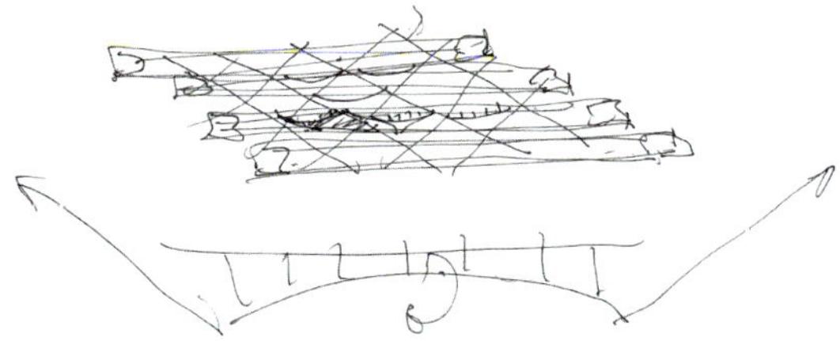

B. GEOMETRIC ELEMENTS

As well as the irregular forms described above, some of OAB's topographic roofs use strict geometric shapes. In these examples, the soft grid of irregular triangles used in the Botanic Garden or the oblongs of Granada and Castelló were transformed into a network of equilateral triangles. The design for the **ZARAGOZA INTERMODAL STATION** (2001–03) was not a matter of adapting or imitating a given topography but instead entailed introducing light into the huge station and giving the gigantic roof a sense of lightness. The enormous diagonal beams cross other beams at the base of the roof, creating a grid of equilateral triangles. In this project, designed a few years after the Botanic Garden, Ferrater used the same successful resource of raising the corners of some of these discrete elements. This time, however, his aim was to create enormous skylights that transform the huge roof, which could have been oppressive, into a transparent filigree.

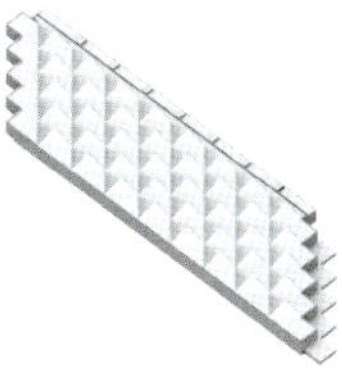

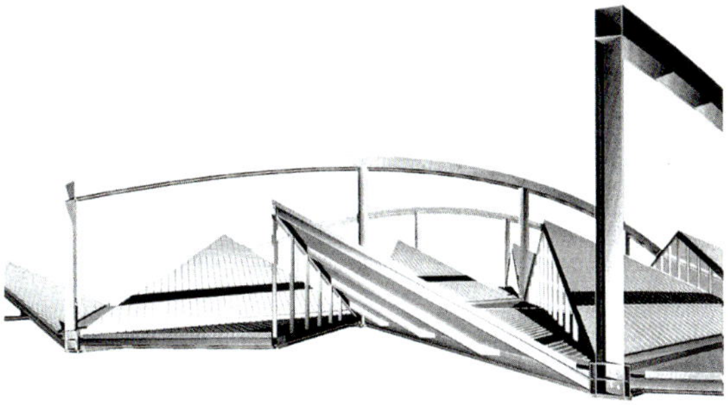

In the design for the **FRONTAURA WINERY** (Toro, Zamora, 2007), which was created almost immediately after the station, Ferrater once again applied a geometric grid to the roof, as in Zaragoza. Here, the roof is broken down into square elements, each of which is divided into two triangles. One of these triangles is turned onto its side, creating a peak that houses two triangular skylights. The network of diagonals of the roof follow the lines of the vines shown in the photo montage of the background of the model.

Sometimes simple resources can be used to evoke movement. On a facade, this can be achieved with basic procedures, as at **THE BARCELONA EDITION HOTEL** (2014–18), where the windows protrude from the building as two flat planes that meet along a vertical apex, with the angles of the frames changing along the facade.

Just as the building work in Zaragoza was completed, OAB began two more housing projects. One of these was in Plaça de **LESSEPS** (Barcelona, 2004–07). This design was Ferrater's first attempt at applying a grid to a facade. Breaking it down into discrete, repeated elements mimics the process of creating an elevation in an architectural design. Manipulating each component in this way and rotating it sideways can breathe life into a facade. In this case, the facade is broken down into two superimposed grids—the outer one is made up of shutters and railings and the inner one by glazing. The elements of the outer grid slant off in pairs from one of their edges, while the grid of windows slants inward, opening up some pleasant intermediate spaces or shuttered terraces. The architects continued using grids and manipulating the different parts of these to create the appearance of the facade and make it functional.

Similar resources were used in the **VÉRTIX HOUSING DEVELOPMENT** (Barcelona, 2003–07). The principle is the same: displacing each of the elements that make up the two layers of the facade. The result here is a little more complex, though, because the outer layer has the added freedom of the broken line, which introduces variety into the elevation and the intermediate spaces. The brilliant result adds a spectacular vertical perimeter void to the city skyline.

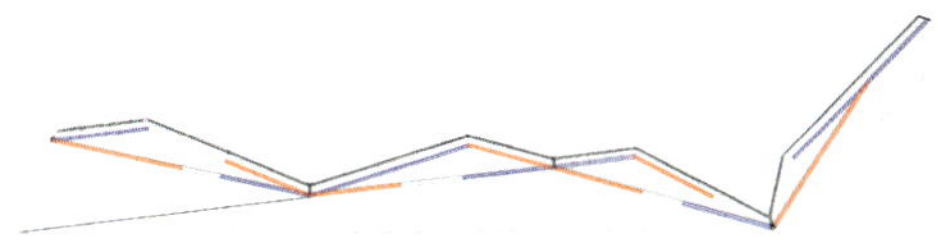

"The designs presented in this chapter experiment with the intermediate space that forms on the threshold between the inside and outside areas of each home. The shutters fold in on themselves, creating a space that filters out the weather, enabling residents to regulate their privacy and control the amount of light they let in, creating outdoor spaces that are an extension of the home. José Antonio Coderch de Sentmenat had already played with this approach in his 1955 housing development for fishermen in Barceloneta, beside the port of Barcelona."

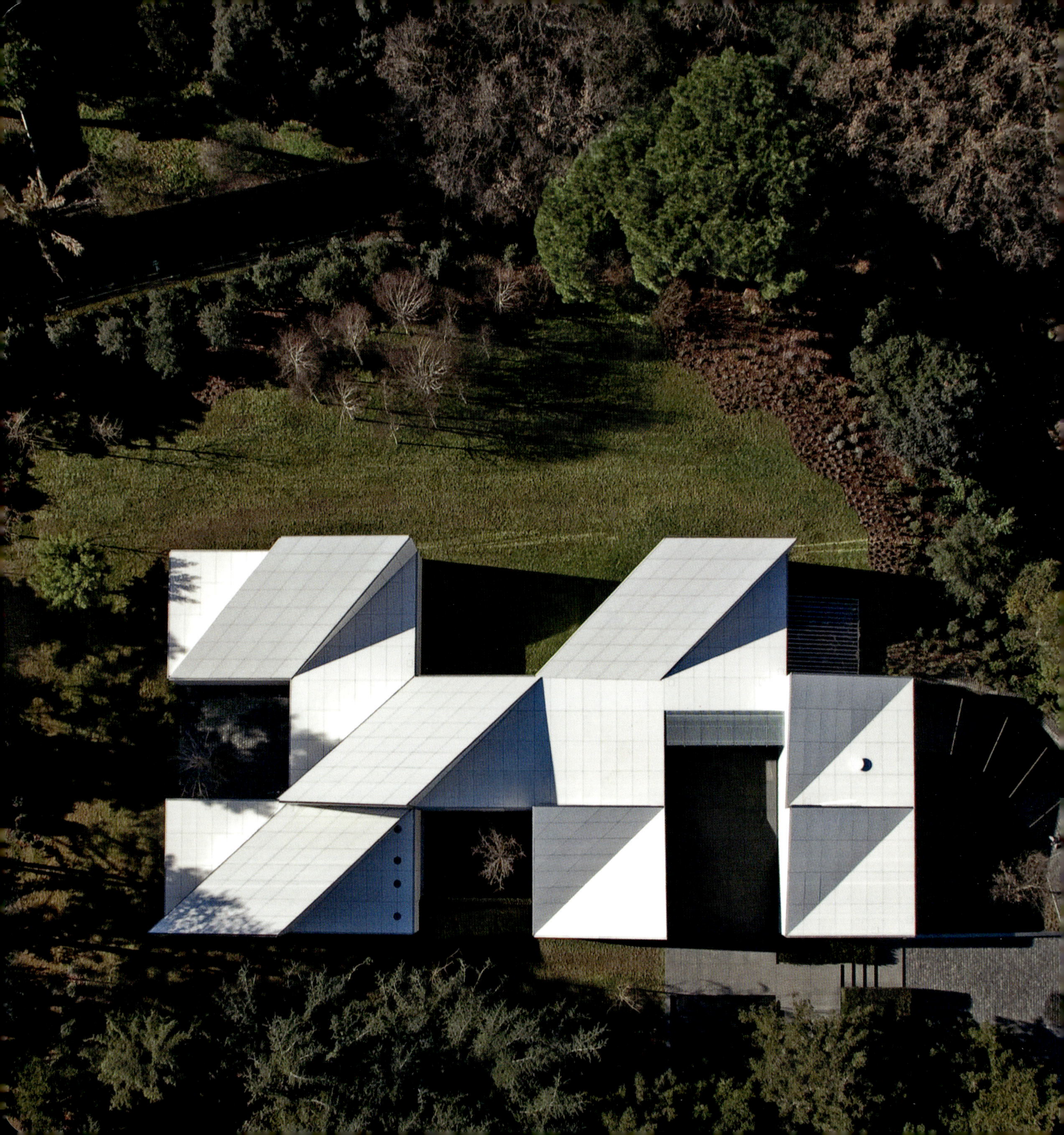

The architects describe the **AA HOUSE** (Sant Cugat, 2009–11) as follows:

"The house follows basic geometric rules that are so simple they give rise to a truly powerful design. As with La Ricarda, one of Antoni Bonet Castellana's iconic designs, the AA House is based on a logic of aggregating squares, but in this case, the geometric order is based on the diagonals of the roofline, making the building a single geometric unit and unifying the interior and the exterior. The 45-degree diagonals lift up sections of the roof, some of which contain skylights and higher ceilings, creating an artificial topography that towers over the site."

This extract from the project report makes it clear that the use of a grid of discrete elements is more rigid and regular in this design, which began with a modular base of 7 x 7-meter squares. These squares form rhombuses and triangles when they are intersected by the long diagonals that reach across the entire building. These flat shapes are raised on one side, creating the choppy effect of the roof. Carlos and Xavier even insisted on reminding us here of the topographical origin of their approach.

This complex structure with its large spans was made technically possible by using a 20-centimeter-thick post-stressed concrete slab that could rest on scattered supports and be raised in the sections with higher ceilings. The photograph shows how hard it was to create this slab.

Ultimately, the geometric mechanism used was exactly the same as at the Botanic Garden: division into discrete elements, which were then manipulated. But the AA House is not in the least organic. The elements into which the grid is broken down are absolutely regular and they are all rotated at the same angle.

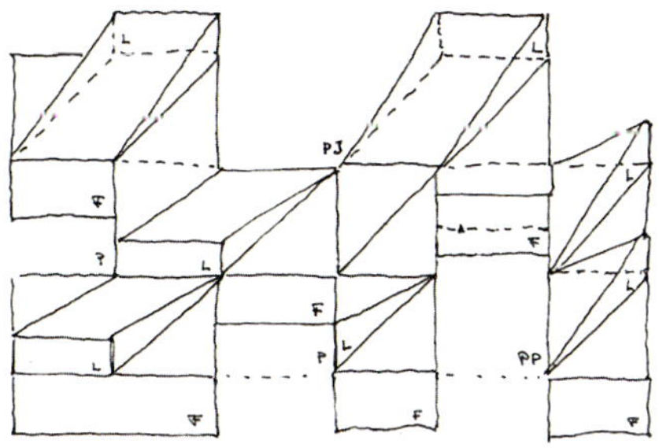

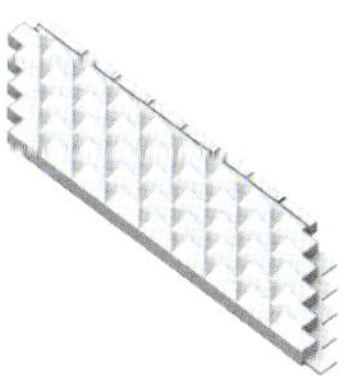

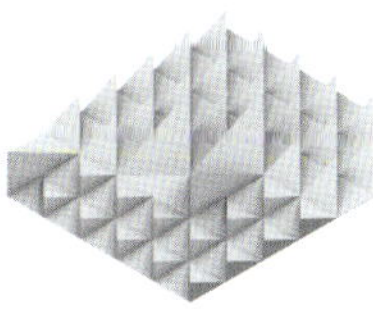

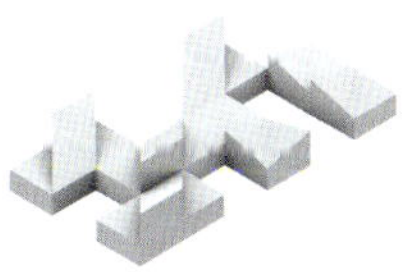

V. DISPLACEMENT OF LINES TO FORM A GENERATRIX

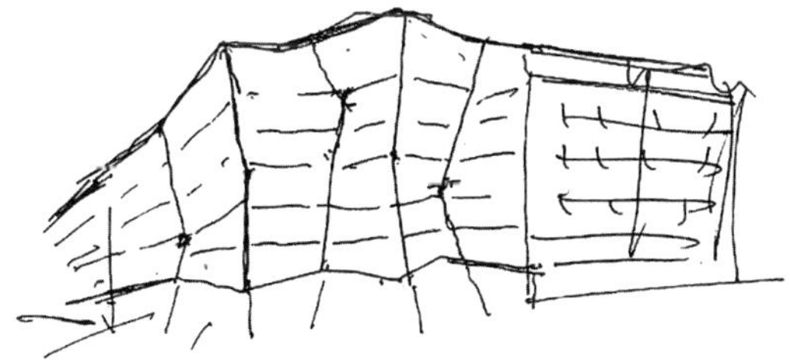

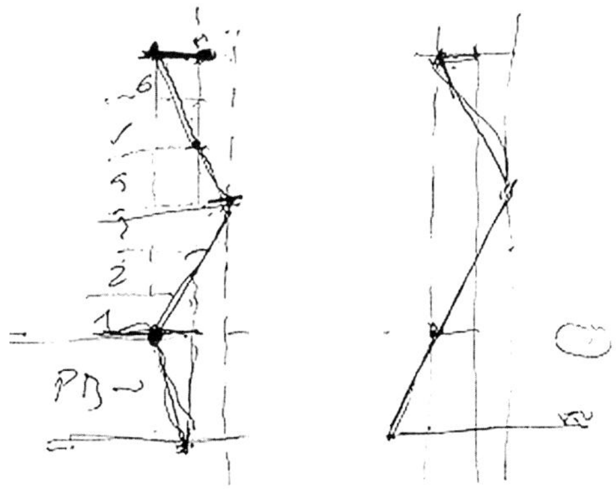

It is harder to summarize what the designs in this section have in common, but the idea undoubtedly originates in the same principles as the two previous classifications: the breaking up of a mainly vertical surface into horizontal bands or strips.

Suppose that, as in the Botanic Gardens, we start to push some of these strips to deform the whole shape. If this displacement is caused by straight or broken vertical lines that push the surface inwards or outwards, we will obtain a drawing like Carlos's design for the **HOUSING DEVELOPMENT ON THE CHAMFER IN PASSEIG DE GRÀCIA** (2000–04). Unfortunately, this idea remained on the drawing board.

This approach opens up possibilities that have not yet been greatly explored. In this case, the lines used to alter the surface of the grid are absolutely free.

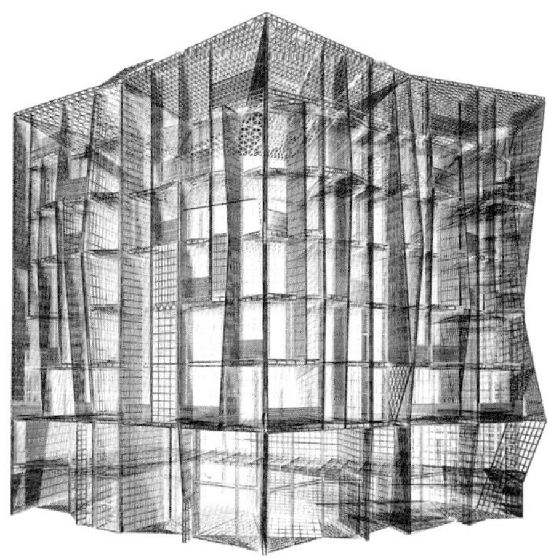

In the housing development in Plaça de Lesseps, the vertical surface was broken down into squares or rectangles that were rotated in an orderly fashion, keeping the vertical lines straight. This design is much more complex because the lines are not continuous, vertical, or straight, and their broken course changes the surface of the facade much more freely.

The design process was subject to the strict municipal regulations defining projections, rotations, depths, and so on. These geometrical rules were used to create an algorithm that suggested and limited the resulting shapes.

This design was intended to be a 21st-century counterpart for Gaudí's iconic building La Pedrera, which is on the same street, and was a powerful, highly evocative proposal that deserved to make a lasting impact.

However, the purest idea in this somewhat invented category was created and built about a dozen years before the project described above. Suppose we break a vertical sheet down into a series of horizontal strips and that these strips are joined every few meters by rigid vertical lines, which we move by tilting them forward or backward, left or right.

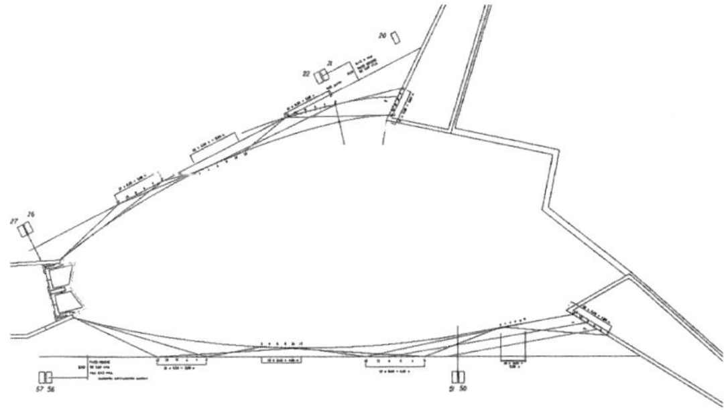

The outcome would be precisely what is shown in the photograph of the lobby of the **JUAN CARLOS HOTEL** (Barcelona, 1989–92), on the right. The fronts of the floor slabs and the parapet walls of each floor make up the horizontal strips described above, and the vertices of the slabs are pushed into different places by the tilting vertical lines.

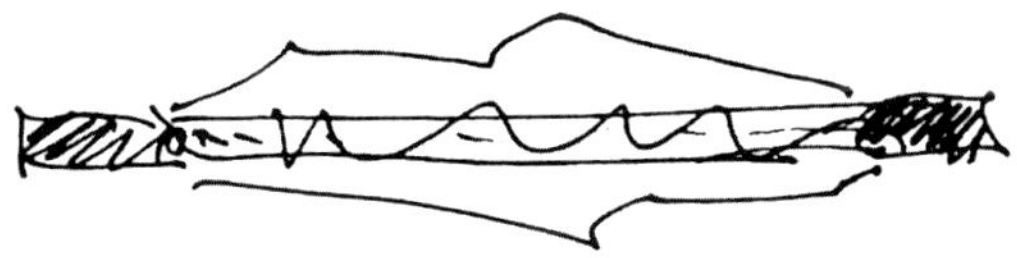

Ferrater used this innovative formula, which was deceptively simple but highly effective, to design the hotel's vast lobby. The edges of the floor slabs form a zig-zagging polygon. But in plan, these lines are slightly but regularly offset from one another. The vertices of the polygon form sloping lines, creating a rich, undulating surface that surprises and impresses visitors.

As before, these shapes are the result of geometric manipulations, but the approach owes to an economical approach to the construction process. It is difficult to create a shape as varied and evocative as this merely by repeating slab edge formwork with minor displacements between one floor and the next.

The work is from 1989–1992, a very creative time for Ferrater, when he also designed the Botanic Garden.

He tested the approach used in the hotel foyer again in 1999 in a spectacular design for a **TOWER BLOCK IN THE 22@ DISTRICT.**

This geometrical resource has also influenced other designs of his, including the **IMQ ZORROTZAURRE HOSPITAL** (Bilbao, 2010–2012).

A couple of interesting outsiders should also be included in this group of geometric manipulations. The first of these is a competition design for a **MUSEUM IN LYON** (2000). I will return to the design process for this project later, but it is contemporary to that of the housing development on the chamfer in Passeig de Gràcia, which it resembles. Various broken vertical planes were displaced with respect to one another to create uncovered outdoor spaces.

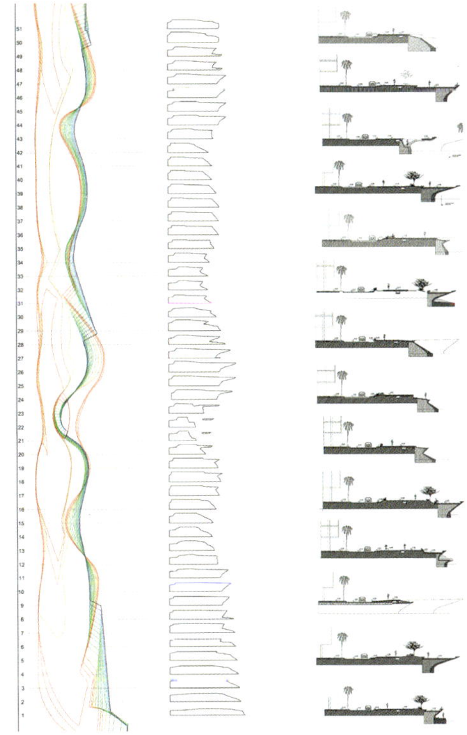

The **BENIDORM SEAFRONT** (2005–09) was designed and built a few years later. Its inclusion in this group is not self-evident: the resulting shape differs substantially from those described above because it is the only case in which the line that is displaced to create the vertical surface is a free curve. Ferrater had almost no choice but to seek out a sensual form to design the area dividing the town of Benidorm from its southern beach.

The outcome is a containing wall that resolves the difference in the heights of the promenade and the beach itself. The front of the wall is a geometrically varied surface whose overall shape is reminiscent of a wave, not just because of its sinuous form but also because it projects over itself like a vast concrete breaker.

This surface could be said to have been generated by displacing a variable curved line moving along an undulating course running parallel to the coastline. The only two conditions for this movement were that the resulting surface should be continuous and that it could be built in wood by breaking it down into a series of formworks.

The combination of undulations along the route and the variable curvature of the line of the wall produces an amazing variety of spatial configurations. All manner of corners are possible. The different colors used in the upper section add to the sensuality of the project.

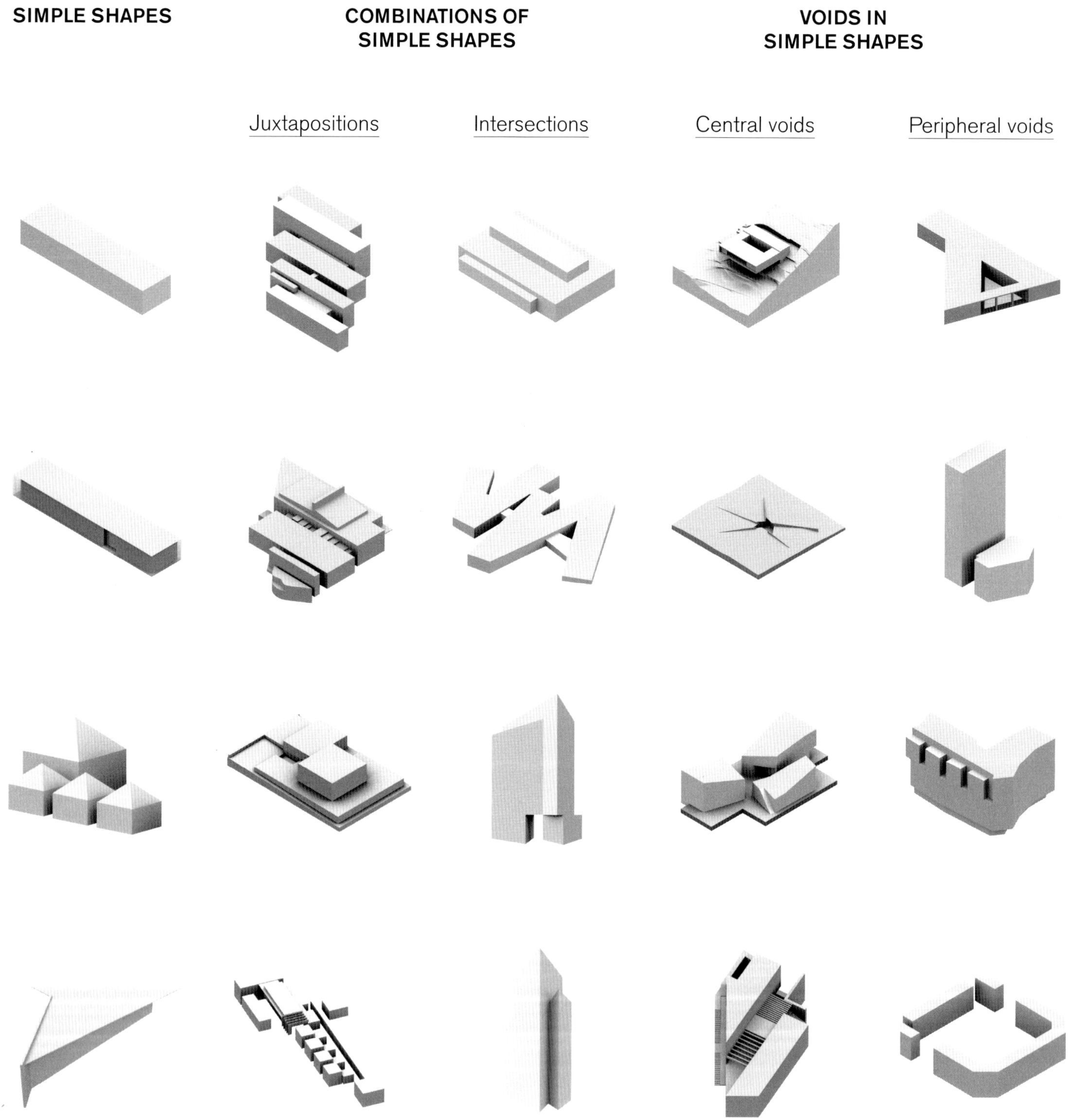

3D icons of the main Taxonomy projects

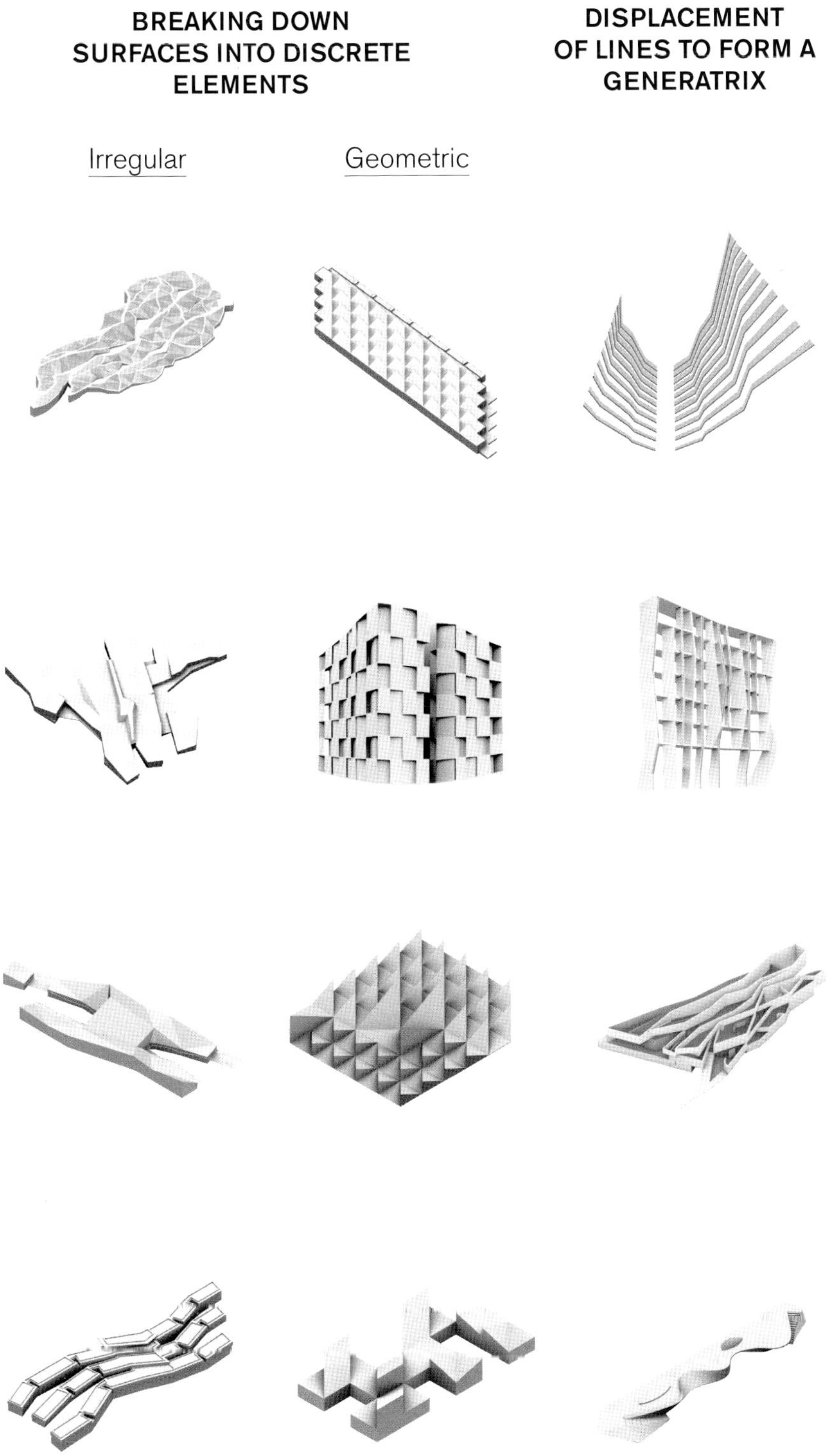

The table summarizes the taxonomy described in the first section of the book.

The shapes in columns 1, 2, and 3 are manipulations of simple volumes that are almost always prismatic and that have a long tradition in the history of architecture. What is makes Ferrater's approach to them exceptional is his systematic exploration of each of these resources and, above all, his use of geometric manipulation from the very start of the design process, making it a tool for solving functional problems, for adapting designs to the site, or for architectural expression.

In columns 4, 5, and 6, the role of geometry as the guiding force behind each design is even more powerful, as these projects involve relatively superficial elements that acquire volume through the design process, regardless of whether the surfaces in question are roofs or facades. These three categories have something else in common: the surfaces are broken down into discrete elements, and various kinds of distortions are applied to them. The elements in column 6 fairly irregular, but those of column 7 are more regular and their geometry is more imposing. Finally, the surfaces in column 8 are grids with differing levels of elasticity on which bands or strips are drawn. Other elements are then added: in a couple of cases, these are straight lines that move, deforming the elastic surface, bringing a third dimension with spectacular results. The Benidorm project is included in this column because it also entails an elastic surface that is deformed, but in this case, the lines used are entirely free curves. Almost all these designs originated in the Botanic Garden, which was undoubtedly the starting point for most of Carlos Ferrater's more recent innovations in form.

2. GEOMETRY IN THE DESIGN PROCESS

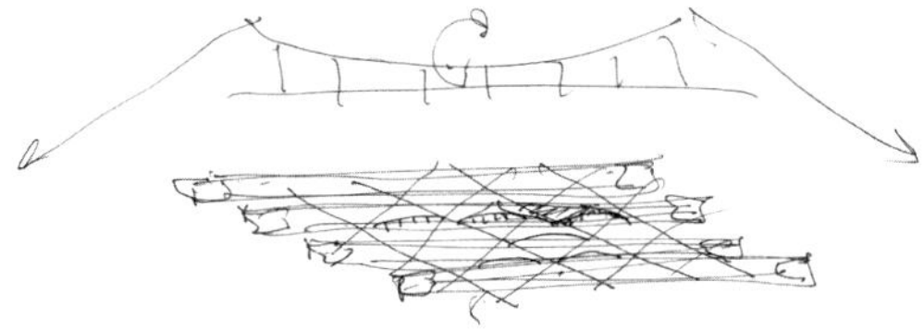

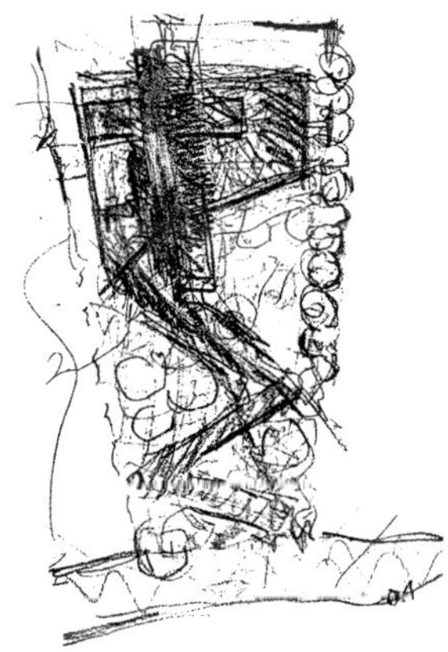

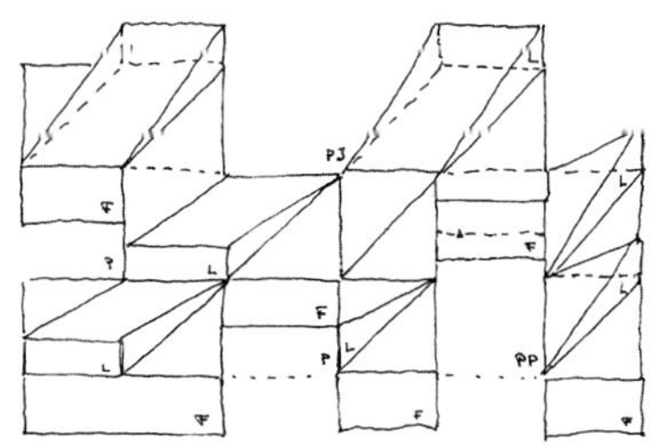

After the brief and the site have been studied, the design process begins to come together: the confusion of forms can be brought into order using geometry. Geometry suggests approaches and strategies and, as these take shape, it becomes the guiding principle for how to handle them.

All architects manipulate shapes in the design process, but few do so while imposing strict geometric rules on themselves in the way that Carlos Ferrater does. For this reason, to a certain extent, his work can be understood as a return to the geometric rigor of classical composition. It could be described a classical but with modern forms or, as he likes to put it, it uses classical syntax with a modern vocabulary.

I get the impression that once the site and the functional brief have been studied and volumes begin to emerge that tie these functions down and locate them on the site, the OAB architects always pay a great deal of attention to the suggestions that arise from geometry. In implementing these suggestions, they adhere strictly to the rules that the discipline imposes. The exhibition that served as a catalyst for this text also included a sample of the initial sketches for the works on display. When seen together, on the opposite page, they seem to suggest two approaches. Some contain light, graceful, simple lines that show the essential elements of the design (the Zaragoza Intermodal Station or the Children's Holiday Center, for example). However, the insistent pencil strokes of some of the geometric drawings suggest that the sketch involved a furious struggle (the MediaPro Building, the Alonso Planas House). The simple sketch of the AA House looks like something Ferrater might have drawn once the project was already well underway. It is impossible to speculate on the role these drawings played in the design process because it is not clear when they were made. Carlos is the first to quote Alejandro de la Sota: *"Not a single line on paper until the design is complete in your head."*

In the next section, I examine how Ferrater uses geometry at different times and in three different ways:

- **–As a suggestion at the beginning of a design**
- **–To guarantee rigor**
- **–As a design tool**

I. AS A SUGGESTION AT THE BEGINNING OF THE DESIGN

Geometry is a *suggestion* because any geometric image can become the matrix for a design. But these suggestions can take many different forms and may be specific and targeted or more generic.

A. OTEIZA'S CHALK MODELS

I have no doubt that the relationships Ferrater created between the boxes at the Impiva Technology Park, and perhaps in some other designs in which prisms are juxtaposed, are linked to sculptor Jorge Oteiza's Chalk Laboratory, a studio which Ferrater visited in Navarre. "My Chalk Laboratory, which forces me to think visually and behave myself. Pure logic," as the sculptor put it.

"Between 1957 and 1974, Jorge Oteiza worked in the Chalk Laboratory, a small experimental space where he tested spatial prototypes made with small plaster prisms. This work formed the basis for much of his later work. The methodological intensity of the studio has been a source of inspiration in the history of art and architecture, and it has become a benchmark for research due to how Oteiza's rigorous, intensive, elemental work was grounded in science." This quotation from Antonio Juárez, a lecturer at ETSAM, perfectly illustrates how inspiring this collection of miniature sculptures is.[4]

"I had always admired Oteiza's insect-like persistence," Ferrater says. In some of his pieces for the Cemex research group at Monterrey Institute of Technology and Higher Education in Mexico, which he collaborated with for many years, Ferrater's designs looked like the chalk pieces from Oteiza's laboratory, showing the importance of this as a lasting source of inspiration over the years.

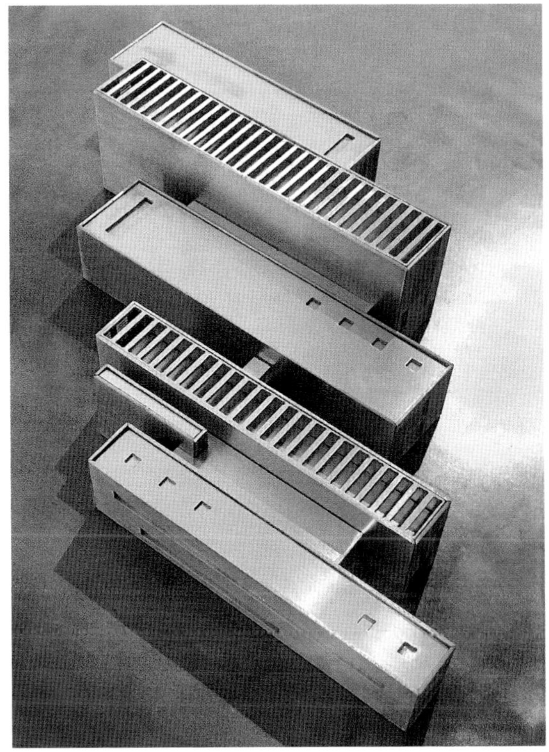

B. PICASSO AND THE HOUSE AT ALCANAR

Sometimes evocative geometry comes from other disciplines, such as painting. Carlos Ferrater associates the design for the House for a Photographer II with Picasso's Cubist paintings of Horta de Sant Joan, which are regarded as the first Cubist works.

"The starting point for the house at Alcanar was a stereotypical plan for two people, but I was looking for an idea to base the design on and give me an alibi, as it were, for it. I let the weeks go by and, during a visit to Paris, I went to the Picasso Museum, where I discovered a picture by the artist painted at Horta de Sant Joan, which is near the house site." [5]

Ferrater sketched the design shown here there and then, in one of his wife's notebooks.

The interesting thing is the immediate affinity with the early Cubist language of Picasso, who was one of the first to interpret the spirit of the Mediterranean. Picasso spent three months in Horta during his second stay there in 1908, when he painted various landscapes.

The painting Carlos saw in Paris was *Factory in Horta de Sant Joan*, described in the French version as a "briqueterie." I've included another picture painted at the same time: *Houses on a Hill.* Its geometric shapes are even more uncompromisingly Cubist and very similar to those that were used in the final design for the house. The relationship between these shapes even gives rise to dark, attractive, intermediate spaces like those in the house. That year, the critic Louis Vauxcelles described the compositions as "bizarreries cubiques" [cubic curiosities]. In fact, for Picasso, these shapes were not cubes, but rather the open faces of a three-dimensional volume.

C. JOANET'S PIECES OF CARDBOARD

The most transparent and attractive example of this first approach comes from the architect's own comments on his entry for the competition to design a Museum in Lyon (2000). The starting point was an entirely abstract model consisting of pieces of cardboard that were brought into the studio one day by a young architect who had recently joined the firm.

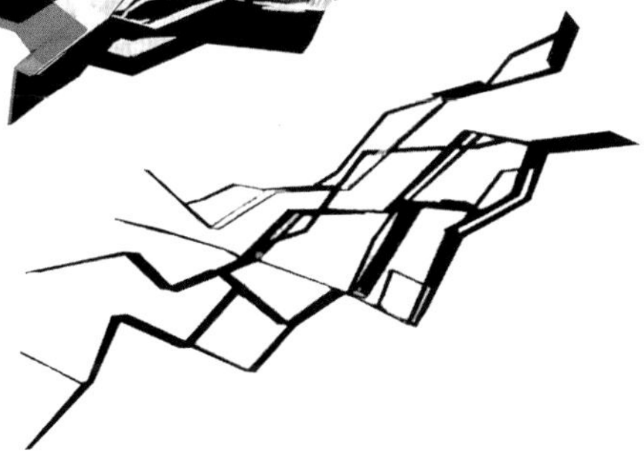

"One weekend we held a little competition in the studio. We wanted to see who could bring a small object or drawing on Monday that could become the leitmotiv for the design. We all brought something in and put them on a table... One of them was a little model made of cardboard strips. I asked, 'So, who made that?' It had been brought in by a young architect called Joanet Rodríguez who'd only been at the studio a week. He was really shy. We asked him what he planned to do with it. He said he hadn't planned to do anything with it, he'd just put together some bits of cardboard and it had come out like that. 'Well, that cardboard thing isn't bad,' I said. 'Come on! Let's see what happens if we carry on with it and really do something with those bits of cardboard'." [6]

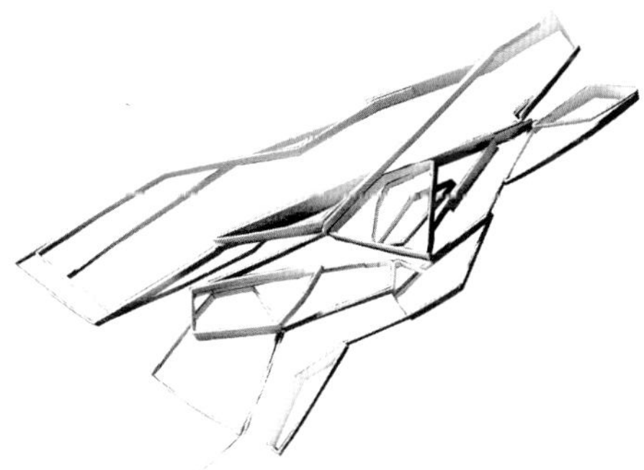

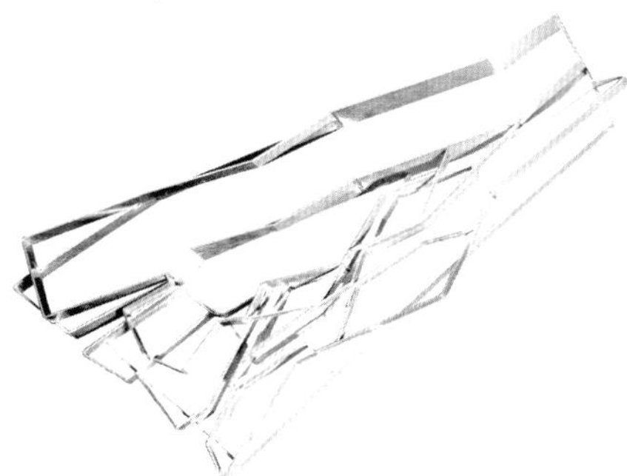

The top right-hand picture shows Joanet's cardboard model. Underneath are three of the models that were subsequently made, first in cardboard, then in plastic, and finally in aluminum. The picture at the bottom is the final design.

The studio took up the idea and worked on it until it met all the design objectives.

The system brings together all the complex aspects of the brief. While the structure reflects the issues of erosion and sedimentation, the museum's folded walls create a complex geometry with infinite possible variations, always obeying the laws of formation.

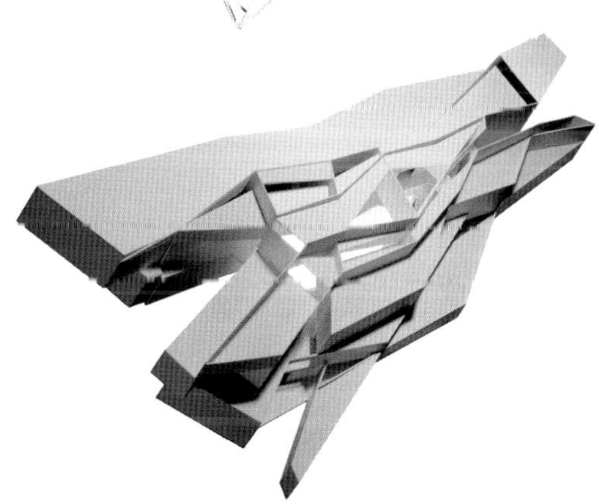

II. TO GUARANTEE RIGOR

Geometry can be used to guarantee rigor because it has its own laws. It enters into dialogue with the functional, technical and aesthetic objectives, but ultimately imposes its own order. The thing about Euclid's geometry is that once a law of formation has been adopted, the whole design progresses subject to that law.

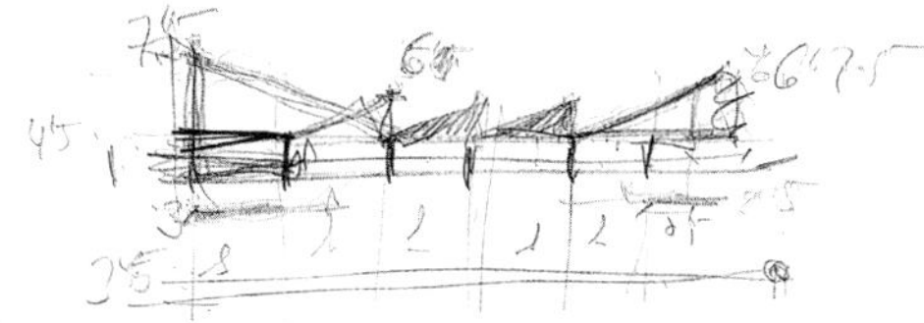

A. THE PAINFUL PROCESS OF ACHIEVING RIGOR

The design process for the AA House discussed above is an example of how rigorous the laws of geometry can be. The plan is very simple. A few squares are juxtaposed, forming courtyards and recesses. A few diagonals appear on this plan, sometimes crossing various squares. One of the triangles into which a square is divided is flipped up onto one of its sides, its apex forming a sloping roof and allowing large skylights to be included. If the triangles are always rotated the same way, the volume of the whole building will be determined by the initial geometric decisions. The crests are as tall as geometry requires them to be. As with origami, the limits are clear. Some spaces are in danger of being too high—there is a risk of some of the attics not being in the most useful locations. All this will have to be agreed on and adjusted, but ultimately geometry will lay down the law. These difficult decisions are not the fault of the architect adopting the standard strategy of manipulating the discrete elements of a grid. What has brought us to this point was the initial approach: using a rigid plan made up of equal squares. When this plan was converted to triangles that were lifted following a single law of rotation, it defined the entire shape of the project.

"Xavi and I have enjoyed ourselves, but we have also had a hard time. By adding these diagonals, all the edges come together. The geometry is very clear, but at the same time it's hellish because the columns have to be eccentric because the outer surface needs to be smooth."[8]

Achieving rigor tends to be a painful process.

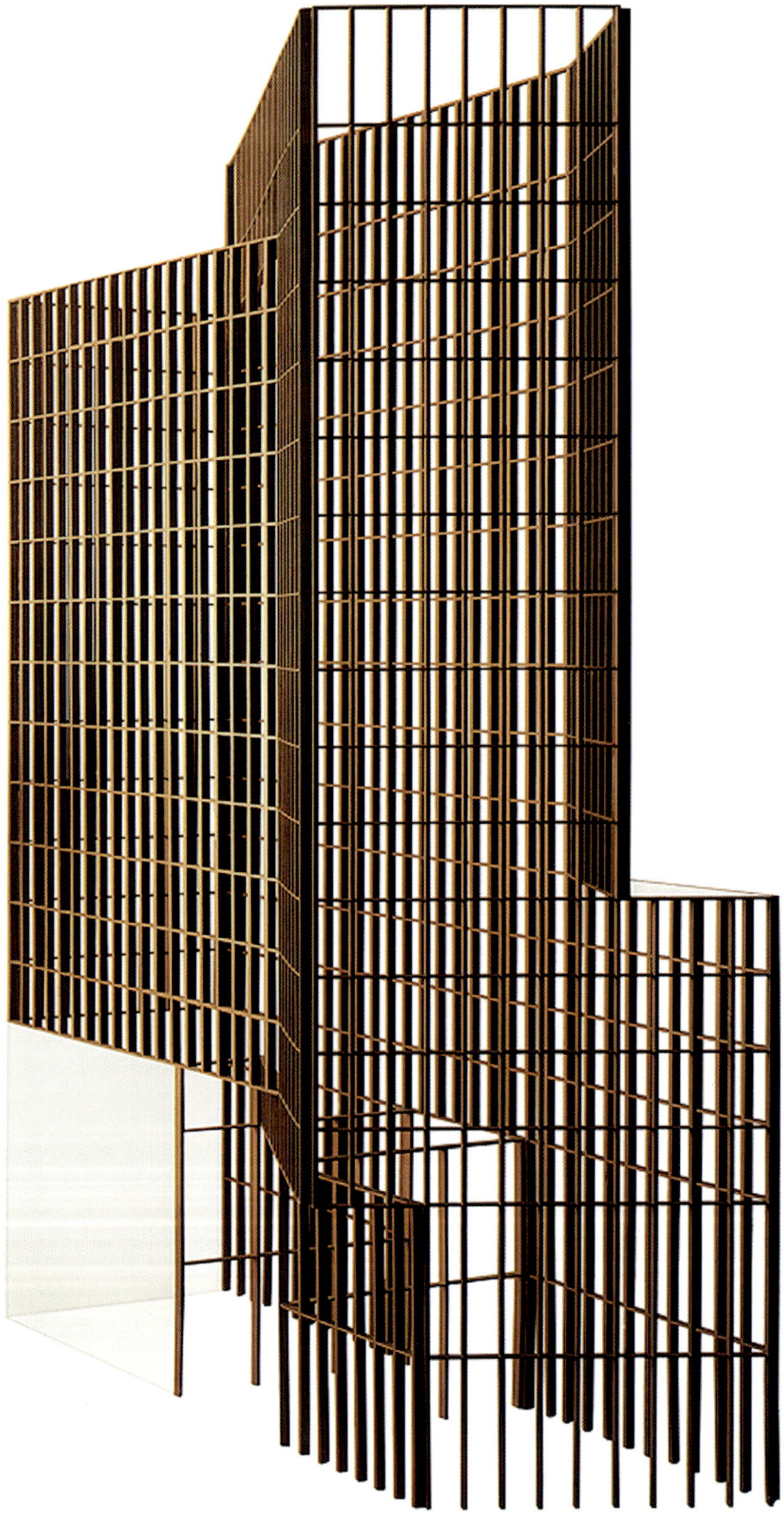

B. MEDIAPRO: THE HOMOGENEOUS GRID

The MediaPro Building was an important project for OAB. Ferrater has said that it was the result of four or five years of experimenting with his designs.[9]

This building is imposing. The clarity of the forms that run parallel to the different streets flanking it contribute to this power, as does the repetition in the facade, which provides almost all the structural support for the building.

"A standard floor has 74 pillars that are spaced between 1.9 m and 2.05 m apart, depending on how the length of each facade divides up. The appearance is one of absolute regularity. The pillars are made up of a steel casing filled with super-plasticized concrete to make it more fire resistant.

"All the pillars have an outside perimeter of 60 cm x 30 cm. All that varies is the thickness of the steel casing, depending on the load each pillar is bearing. Some of them are solid steel." [10]

In fact, as shown in the diagram, the pillars around the four-story opening bear loads of up to 12 tons. This is about three times the average for the pillar type used most in the design. However, these pillars look the same size as all the others, as can be seen in the model here.

I have gone into some detail in this explanation to show the design, calculation, and construction efforts needed to achieve such a powerful sense of order, how rigor is embodied in a load-bearing facade.

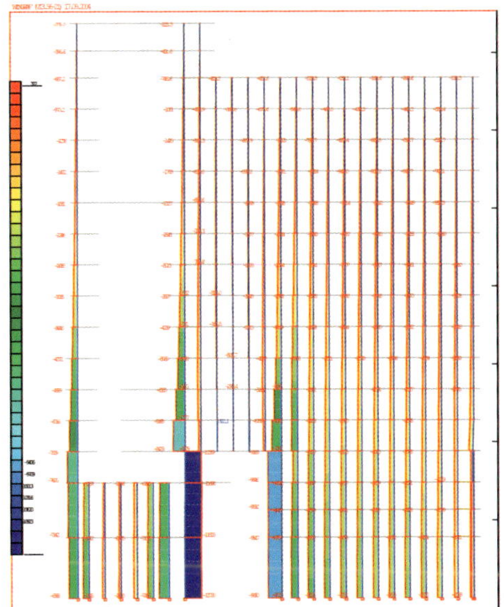

SIMULACIÓN DE AXILES EN LOS PILARES

C. ISOTROPIC CORNERS

The construction process conjures up lines and directionality, particularly if frame-based construction systems are used. The most powerful examples of this are railway stations, a succession of porticoes that are open at the front. Nothing could be more directional or more anisotropic.

"Isotropic" and "anisotropic" are terms most often used in mineralogy, to describe the directionality and characteristics of crystals. When crystals expand equally in the two directions of the plane, they are called isotropic.

The purest forms of architecture tend not be anisotropic—centrality is what makes a monumental building. Extremely simple forms like the sphere, and, failing that, the cube or the cylinder, are supreme examples of geometric perfection and are the most isotropic of shapes. For prisms to approach such isotropy, the walls on the shorter sides must be handle in the same way as the longer ones. When the facade reaches the corners joining them, it should continue round them without interruptions.

What tricks Mies van de Rohe had to pull off at the Crown Hall, for example, to make an entirely directional framed structure appear to be isotropic! I discussed this in greater detail in an article published in *AV* (no. 6, 1986).

Ferrater and his team began their quest for this kind of isotropy as far back as 1982, in the design for the Sports Center in Torroella de Montgrí. The frame is supported by columns that also hold up the edge beam and are identical to the ones bearing the internal floor beams across a huge span, as can be seen through the glass in the photo.

They have continued to seek isotropy in many other buildings. At the Vila-real Library, the envelope of ceramic bars curves round, forming a symmetrical corner. At the Roca Gallery, it is the magnificent pieces of laminated glass that are repeated in the facade and the frame. At Casa SEAT, the glass of the facade bends around the corner, where the metal framework has been removed to give absolute continuity to the two facades.

III. AS A DESIGN TOOL

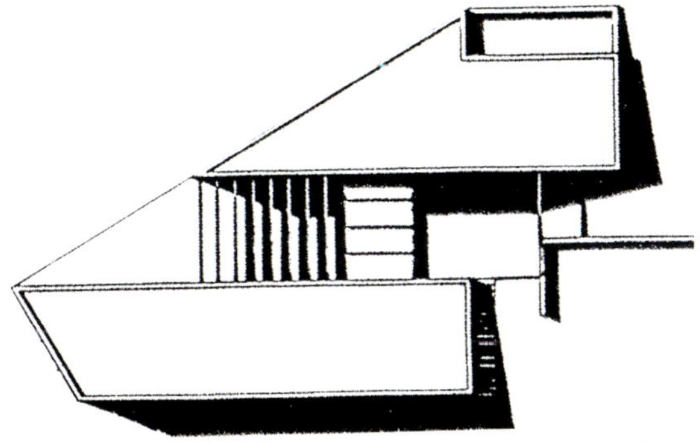

The use of geometry as a tool during the design process is an integral part of Carlos Ferrater's work. Many of the manipulations discussed in this book arose as ingenious strategies to resolve specific design problems.

A. THE TRIGINER HOUSE: THE "CHOP"

In some cases, the volumetrics of the design need to be interfered with handle difficult functions and topographies, as at the Triginer House:

"Jordi showed me the site, which was undoubtedly the worst of the five or six plots resulting from the division of a splendid property that literally hangs above the city of Barcelona. The plot had barely five meters of frontage, which was the only access point, and there was a slope of more than 60 percent. It took me 14 months to call the client to tell him I didn't feel able to go ahead with the project." [11]

The joy of the owner, who assumed Carlos was calling him to tell him he had finished the plans, left him feeling incapable of pulling out, and he agreed to present something three days later.

"I shut myself in the studio that weekend. After going over and over it, I didn't so much see a solution as come up with one through intuition, and, like Alexander with the Gordian knot, I chopped right through the center of the drawing, making a courtyard—an empty space running right through the plot from north to south. From then on, with the center empty, the house started to work." [12]

Putting in a wide, unroofed passage through the center of the site solved the problems of distribution and topography, enabling a central access point via the upper floor. At the Década Awards ceremony, Glenn Murcutt said: *"The architect has created a platform on the first floor which connects the main parts of the house. This is a deceptively simple solution on the most difficult of sites."* In this case, the void was the geometric tool that provided the solution.

B. THE BOTANIC GARDEN: A DUCTILE GRID

In some cases, geometry is the overall design strategy. In the case of the Botanic Garden, by superimposing a grid of irregular triangles on the site, Ferrater was able to organize the whole detailed display of plants from around the world, grouped by altitude and climate regions. It is the discrete, triangular elements of the grid that gave rise to these beds and the banks, walls, squares, and paths.

"It was probably the most exciting time of my life, trying things out after the experience with the Botanic Garden: laying a grid on the ground and making it work. At that time, I didn't actually know how far it had worked but I felt it had... The grid stood up to everything... I don't know if it was a coincidence or sheer desperation, probably desperation... but that discovery encouraged me to say that we had to try things out and experiment more, and that we had to innovate. Because there might be ways to go beyond the Modern movement that would blaze new trails and open up new forms of expression. That's what an architect is always looking for."[14]

The design has often been described as fractal in that it clearly is broken into pieces. However, this description doesn't entirely chime with the official definition: fractals contain similar structures on different scales, organized hierarchically. If they are identical, we speak of self-similarity or scale invariance.

However, it was the person who introduced the concept of fractals, Benoit Mandelbrot, who first suggested that Carlos Ferrater was the best example of the use of fractals in Catalonia, in a conversation on Eduard Punset's television show *Redes.*[15]

ROADS AND WALLS UNDER CONSTRUCTION

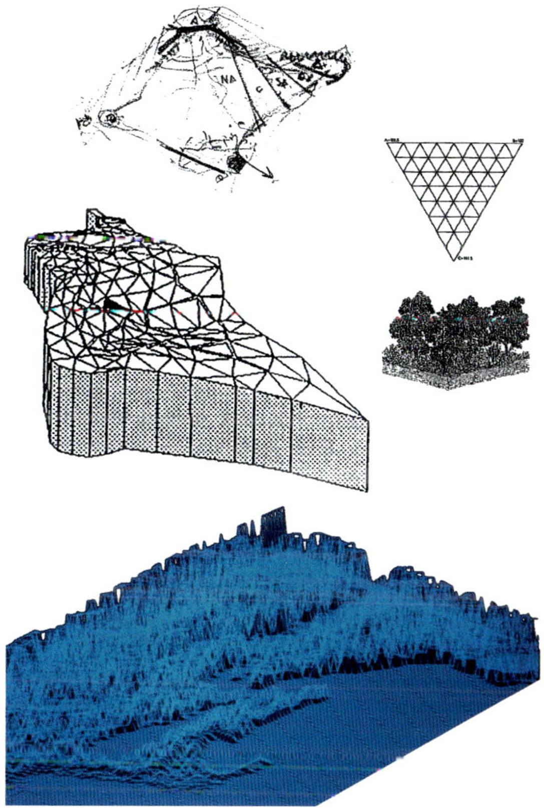

TOPOGRAPHIC HANDLING
Elevation of the vertices

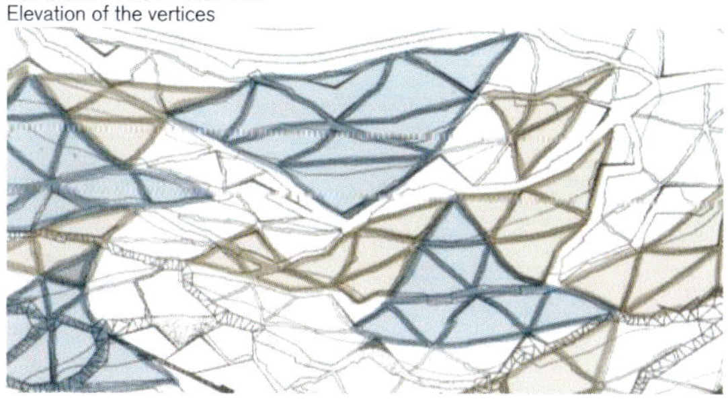

FRACTAL OBJECTS AND ARCHITECTURE
Final Degree Project ETSAV - Celia Ana Martínez Requena

HOTEL
DORADA

III. AS A DESIGN TOOL

C. BENIDORM: TACTILE CONTINUITY

Sometimes the tool is the geometry imposed by the construction technique. At Benidorm, as I discussed a few pages back, the limits of the ship hull carpentry used in the design are what shape the spectacularly varied wave.

The geometry therefore acts as a frame, putting limits on the freehand drawing that offers a host of different situations.

In fact, the architects decided that this time they were going to turn the process around: the formal research would not be guided by computer estimates. Instead, it would be the model that would define the project.[16]

"We then decided to go about things the other way round, which consisted of thinking like a computer and coming up with the geometry manually."

They built a huge 1:10 scale model and made each piece before fitting it with the adjoining pieces, working on the joins manually. As I said, the only limits on the project were that the shape had to be continuous and the frames had to be within the capabilities of the shipbuilding carpenter who would be building them. As long as these conditions were met, freedom of form was possible.

Once the whole seafront had been sculpted, it had to be dismantled, but in a different way, depending on the length of the frame sections that the carpenter was prepared to make and transport. He could then reconstruct the geometry of each frame unit on the computer to make the plans and decide how to break it down for the carpentry process.

Carlos and Xavier rightly see that *"the work of the architect lies in the act of moving from geometry to space."*[9] By stretching the curve of the section along the sinuous line of the plan, Ferrater achieves this sensual geometry, the only precedents for which are Gaudí's containing walls in Park Güell.

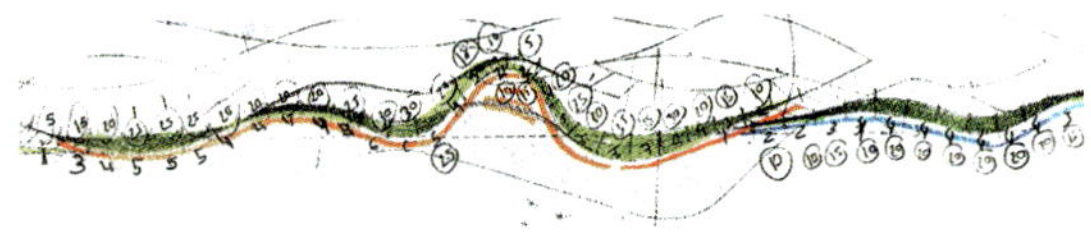

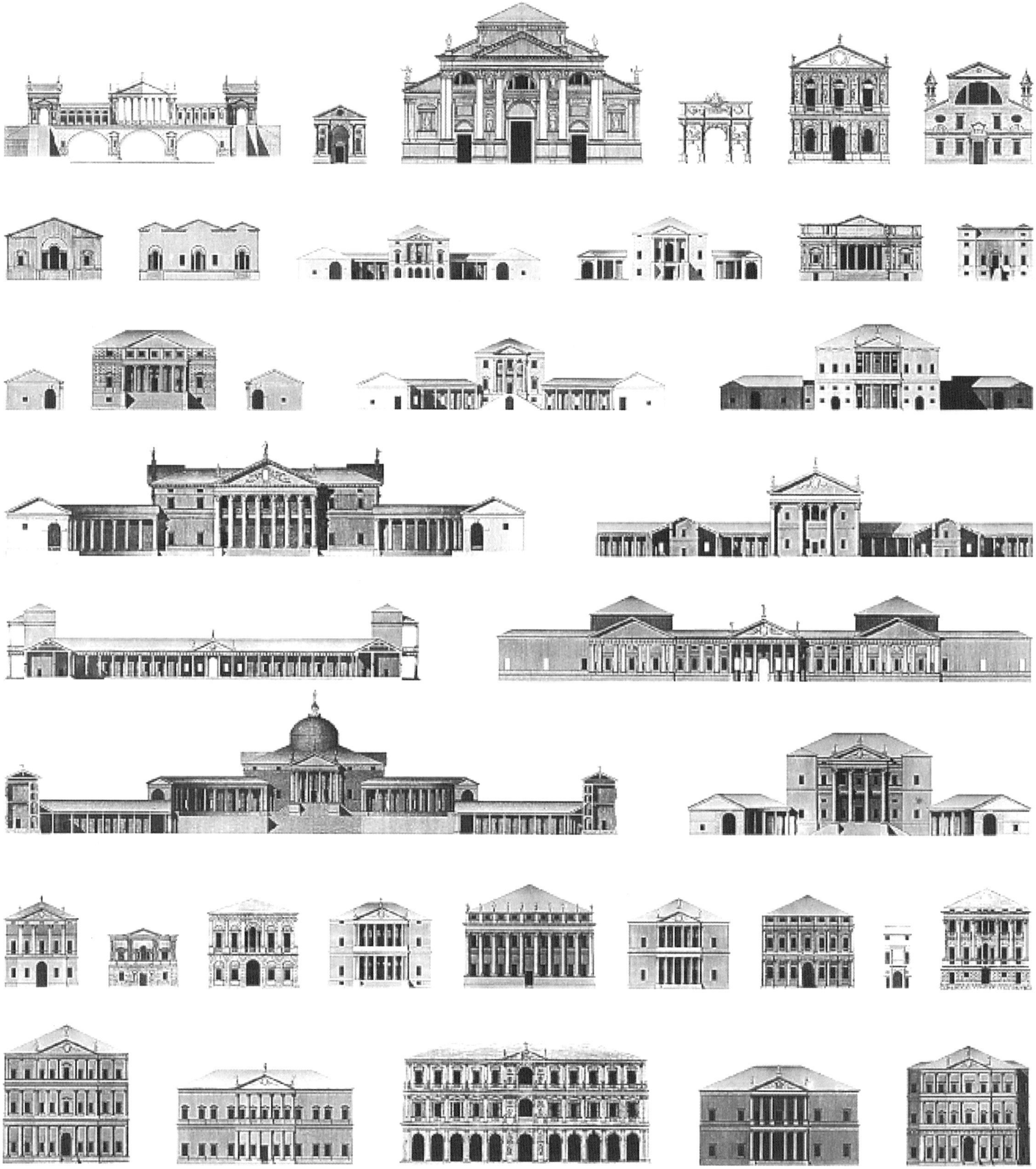

3. GEOMETRY AND COMPOSITION

Composition is the "art of grouping figures and combining the elements required to achieve the most harmonious, balanced work possible" (RAE Spanish dictionary).

I. THE ACADEMIC DEMOLITION OF COMPOSITION AS ANALYSIS OF FORMS

My visit to the collection of models in the Absence of Scale exhibitions conjured up memories of a subject that is no longer taught at architecture schools: analysis and composition of forms. When I took it, we did timid drawing and model-making exercises that were entirely lacking in criteria.

While I was at university, architectural composition (in other words, the typological analysis of architecture through history), disappeared from the degree program. The great treatises, like Durand's, with his taxonomical groupings and geometrical analysis of these shapes, had been standard teaching material until not long before then. At the Barcelona school, this approach was thrown out when a group of fantastic young lecturers brought in new approaches in the 1960s. On one hand, the composition subjects taught by Federico Correa and Helio Piñón were based on commenting on simple design exercises done by the students. On the other, Ignasi Solá-Morales moved toward a form of composition based on analyzing different factors, after which the design was drawn up. This transition was completed when Oriol Bohigas, in his report for the department in 1970, stated "instead of referring to an architectural composition, we need to speak of a theory of design."[15]

But abandoning composition in the sense of the analysis of historical architecture and the classification of geometric manipulations was a serious loss for our education. The close relationship between geometry and composition through typology and history could also be very fruitful. Some of the manipulations I have discussed here had golden ages at different points in history, such as the spectacular Baroque voids or Gothic juxtapositions. Deprived of this kind of training, we architects improvise the composition of our buildings as if each one were the first of its type, not only in history but also in our own catalog of work.

In the series of works I have looked at, I wanted to look for an exploration process, a route through the different resources of geometry to create a working method, perhaps even an extremely subtle theoretical framework for the whole design process.

Bringing together the models at the exhibition we have already mentioned, in which all the buildings exhibited were the same size, reveals Ferrater's insect-like patience in mapping out his career. I wanted to link this effort to traditional composition because I believe this nexus exists. I believe Carlos Ferrater's composition rests on the classical resources of geometry while using an absolutely contemporary vocabulary. My aim has been to link his work with the classical tradition of composition, even though it uses the language of modernity.

Andrea Palladio "Ville, Palazzi e Chiese nel Veneto" 1508-1580

II. GEOMETRY AND THE QUESTION OF STYLE

"Syntax" comes from the Greek "sintassein," which means "to arrange together, to put in order" (RAE Spanish dictionary).

The OAB architects have always wanted to make clear that they are not seeking to create a recognizable style of their own.

"In our work, language has become diluted. In my opinion, language leads to style, and style is the end and the death of architecture. The important thing is syntax, which is the most abstract part of language. Vocabulary, the most figurative part, must be diluted and, at the same time, it must be made more precise." [17]

I believe geometry is the syntax in their work. Geometry is what makes their approach to their different projects coherent. It is the syntax that organizes their forms. Their vocabulary consists of the pure volumes and simple prisms of the Modern movement. That syntax and vocabulary make up what is personal about their work. There is no trace of any desire to make their designs easy to identify by using similar forms. There is no desire to construct a "style."

"By contrast, this other approach is much more closely linked to reality and also to history and the most hidden aspects– everything that is not particularly obvious. This perspective allows you to make each experience new, to start afresh every time, to do away with scale." [18]

Carlos Ferrater feels comfortable with the expression "absence of scale," the name of the exhibition that led me to suggest the idea of this book to him. If the important, essential thing is geometric manipulation, scale is no longer important. The same kinds of interplay and equilibrium are present in the shapes of Oteiza's chalk models as at Impiva, Tagomago, or the Palma de Mallorca City Hall.

"Adopting a clear geometry at the outset, one that can bring intrinsic order to the design, will make it difficult if not impossible for outside factors to intrude. It's a way of armor plating the design process. The fragile beginnings and early stages of creating designs mean we need to preserve them from the management, execution, and implementation processes that often involve noisy equipment that is completely alien to architecture." [19]

Collection of models made with 3D printing for the Exhibition "The absence of scale"

OAB

III. GEOMETRY AS UNIFYING FORCE IN OAB'S WORK. THE ULTIMATE CONTRIBUTION OF GEOMETRY

***Ageometretos medeis eisito*: "Let no-one ignorant of geometry enter." According to tradition, this text appeared above the door of Plato's Academy**

Building a new professional organization has meant years of work. It began with the gradual inclusion of his children, Lucía and Borja Ferrater, and his son-in-law, Xavier Martí. The group moved their studio to the heart of Barcelona, which was emblematic of the firm's identity. In 2006, they founded OAB—Office of Architecture in Barcelona.

This was not just a business move: the team wanted to adopt a strategy for approaching projects that was not a question of style.

"...After these projects, the Botanic Garden in 1989 and those that followed it, the experiments with folds and different geometries continued. We then realized that we had accumulated something of a body of theory based on practice in different projects which allows us to understand design approaches collectively. As geometry is ahierarchical, it makes it possible to divide up group work. And this gave us with a shared working tool that allows us each to work on a story; for us to recruit young specialists to start working on specific projects and for them to keep working for us even if the projects themselves change." [18]

Geometry does not create hierarchies, it is not an imposition, it is a way of bringing things together. When everyone agrees on this approach, it becomes a way for an entire professional team to go about things. Many of the works analyzed here are from the OAB's teamwork period, including substantial contributions from project manager Núria Ayala.

When OAB describes geometry as ahierarchical, I understand that it is alluding to the fact that when all the team members agree to use geometric manipulations as a design tool, they approach this and make use of it on equal terms.[19]

The group has made this way of working its own, as their designs show. Carlos, Xavi, Lucía, Borja, and Núria remind me of Plato's geometricians. They certainly understand geometry, and geometry has the last word in all of OAB's work.

ἀγεωμὲρητος μηδεὶς εἰσίτω

CREDIT LIST OF THE PROJECTS AND WORKS THAT APPEAR IN THE PUBLICATION

TORROELLA DE MONTGRÍ SPORTS CENTER
DATE 1981 - 1985
ARCHITECTS Carlos Ferrater
Jeroni Moner
Arcadi Pla
PHOTOGRAPHY Lluís Casals

EL TERRAT FILM STUDIOS (ARRUGA CINEMA)
DATE 1995-1997
ARCHITECTS Carlos Ferrater
with Joan Guibernau
PHOTOGRAPHY Lluís Casals

ROCA GALLERY
DATE 2008-2009
ARCHITECTS Borja Ferrater
Carlos Ferrater
Lucía Ferrater
PHOTOGRAPHY Alejo Bagué

VILA-REAL LIBRARY
DATE 2009 - 2011
ARCHITECTS Carlos Ferrater
Alberto Peñín
with J. Gimeno
PHOTOGRAPHY Diego Opazo

NEW CITY HALL IN PALMA DE MALLORCA
DATE 2007 - 2007
ARCHITECTS Carlos Ferrater
Núria Ayala

SOCIAL HOUSING IN L'HOSPITALET
DATE 2012 - 2014
ARCHITECTS Carlos Ferrater
Núria Ayala
with Sergi Blanch
and Sandra Rodà

SOCIAL HOUSING IN ECOQUARTIER ANDROMÈDE, TOULOUSE
DATE 2013-2016
ARCHITECTS Carlos Ferrater
Alberto Peñín
PHOTOGRAPHY Joan Guillamat

L'ESTARTIT SAILING CLUB
DATE 1988-1991
ARCHITECTS Carlos Ferrater
Gerardo Rodríguez
Joan Díaz
PHOTOGRAPHY Lluís Casals

CHILDREN'S HOLIDAY CENTER IN VILADOMS
DATE 2010
ARCHITECTS Carlos Ferrater
Núria Ayala
PHOTOGRAPHY Alejo Bagué

REGINA HOUSE
DATE 2019-2020
ARQUITECTO Carlos Ferrater
PHOTOGRAPHY Joan Guillamat

IMPIVA TECHNOLOGY PARK
DATE 1993 - 1995
ARCHITECTS Carlos Ferrater
Carlos Bento
Jaume Sanahuja
PHOTOGRAPHY Lluís Casals

ALONSO PLANAS HOUSE
DATE 1995-1998
ARCHITECTS Carlos Ferrater
Joan Guibernau
PHOTOGRAPHY Lluís Casals

UNIVERSITY LIBRARY AT BELLATERRA
DATE 1998
ARCHITECTS Carlos Ferrater

CATALONIA CONVENTION CENTER
DATE 1996 - 2000
ARCHITECTS Carlos Ferrater
with José Mª Cartañá
and Alberto Peñín
STRUCTURAL ENG. Juan Calvo (Pondio)
PHOTOGRAPHY Alejo Bagué
AERIAL PHOTOGRAPHY Tavisa

EVANGELICAL CHURCH IN TERRASSA
DATE 2007-2010
ARCHITECTS Carlos Ferrater
Lucía Ferrater
PHOTOGRAPHY Alejo Bagué

FISERSA HEADQUARTERS
DATE 1998
ARCHITECTS Carlos Ferrater
PHOTOGRAPHY Lourdes Jansana

TAGOMAGO VILLA
DATE 1999 - 2001
ARCHITECTS Carlos Ferrater
with Joan Guibernau
PHOTOGRAPHY Alejo Bagué

NOLLA HOUSE
DATE 2004 – 2005
ARCHITECTS Carlos Ferrater
with Joan Guibernau
PHOTOGRAPHY Alejo Bagué

F3 HOUSE
DATE 2008 - 2010
ARCHITECTS Lucía Ferrater
Carlos Ferrater
PHOTOGRAPHY Lluís Casals

ANDORRA CASINO
DATE 2017
ARCHITECTS Borja Ferrater
with Carles Gras

SOCIAL SERVICES CENTER AT FORT PIENC
DATE 2001 - 2003
ARCHITECTS Lucía Ferrater
Carlos Ferrater
PHOTOGRAPHY Alejo Bagué

CSIC INSTITUTE BUILDING, BARCELONA BOTANIC GARDENS
DATE 2001 - 2003
ARCHITECTS Carlos Ferrater
PHOTOGRAPHY Alejo Bagué

JOSÉ PÉREZ HOUSING DEVELOPMENT, MADRID
DATE 2002-2005
ARCHITECTS Carlos Ferrater
with Elena Mateu
PHOTOGRAPHY Alejo Bagué

MEDIAPRO BUILDING
DATE 2005-2008
ARCHITECTS Carlos Ferrater
Xavier Martí
Patrick Genard
STRUCTURAL ENG. *Juan Calvo (Pondio)*
PHOTOGRAPHY Alejo Bagué

NEW INCASOL CORPORATE HEADQUARTERS
DATE 2008
ARCHITECTS Carlos Ferrater
with Núria Ayala

HIPPODROME TOWER IN GUADALAJARA
PROYECTO 2012 - 2018
ARCHITECTS Carlos Ferrater
Xavier Martí
PHOTOGRAPHY Alejo Bagué

ARTABRIA ARCHAEOLOGICAL MUSEUM
DATE 2003
ARCHITECTS Carlos Ferrater
with Juan Trias de Bes

BF HOUSE
DATE 2006 - 2011
ARCHITECTS Carlos Ferrater
Xavier Martí
Carlos Escura
Carlos Martín
PHOTOGRAPHY Joan Guillamat

FITNESS CENTER
DATE 1993 - 1996
ARCHITECTS Carlos Ferrater
PHOTOGRAPHY Lluis Casals

HOUSE FOR A PHOTOGRAPHER II IN THE EBRO DELTA
DATE 2003 - 2006
ARQUITECTO Carlos Ferrater
PHOTOGRAPHY Alejo Bagué

CTRIGINER HOUSE
DATE 1996 - 1998
ARCHITECTS Carlos Ferrater
with Joan Guibernau
PHOTOGRAPHY Lluis Casals

KAPLANKAYA CLUBHOUSE
DATE 2012 -2013
ARCHITECTS Carlos Ferrater
Borja Ferrater
PHOTOGRAPHY Joan Guillamat

MODERN ART MUSEUM IN ALMATY, KAZAKHSTAN
DATE 2016
ARCHITECTS Carlos Ferrater
Xavier Martí
Borja Ferrater

MOLINET HOUSE, L'ESTARTIT
DATE 2016
ARQUITECTO Carlos Ferrater
PHOTOGRAPHY Lluís Casals

BINISAFÚA HOUSE
DATE 1988 - 1990
ARCHITECTS Carlos Ferrater
PHOTOGRAPHY Lluís Casals

HOUSE FOR A PHOTOGRAPHER I, LLAMPAIES
DATE 1992-1995
ARCHITECTS Carlos Ferrater
PHOTOGRAPHY Lluís Casals

BUILDINGS AT 109–111 PASSEIG DE GRÀCIA
DATE 2018 - 2020
ARCHITECTS Carlos Ferrater
with Xavier Martí
and Núria Ayala
STRUCTURAL ENG. *Juan Calvo (Pondio)*
PHOTOGRAPHY Joan Guillamat
Alejo Bagué

FIVE BLOCKS ON POBLENOU SEAFRONT
DATE 1989 - 1992
ARQUITECTO Carlos Ferrater
PHOTOGRAPHY Lluís Casals
Joan Guillamat

2 APARTMENT BUILDINGS IN BILBAO
DATE 2005-2011
ARCHITECTS Carlos Ferrater
Xavier Martí
Lucía Ferrater
Luís Domínguez
STRUCTURAL ENG *Juan Calvo (Pondio)*
PHOTOGRAPHY Joan Guillamat

TWELVE HOUSES ON CARRER FERNANDO POO, BARCELONA
DATE 2019
ARCHITECTS Carlos Ferrater
Alberto Peñín
Xavier Martí
PHOTOGRAPHY Joan Guillamat

BARCELONA BOTANIC GARDEN
DATE 2007 - 2008
ARCHITECTS Carlos Ferrater
Bet Figueras
José Luís Canosa
PHOTOGRAPHY Alejo Bagué

SCIENCE MUSEUM AND PARK IN GRANADA
DATE 2004-2008
ARCHITECTS Carlos Ferrater
Eduardo Jiménez
Yolanda Brasa
STRUCTURAL ENG. *Juan Calvo (Pondio)*
PHOTOGRAPHY Alejo Bagué

AZAHAR GROUP HEADQUARTERS
DATE 2007-2009
ARCHITECTS Carlos Ferrater
Núria Ayala
PHOTOGRAPHY Alejo Bagué

URBAN PLANNING FOR GARELLANO
DATE 2009
ARCHITECTS Carlos Ferrater
Luis Domínguez
with Núria Ayala

KAPLANKAYA SIX SENSES WELLNESS RESORT
DATE 2012 - 2016
ARCHITECTS Carlos Ferrater
Borja Ferrater
with Juan Trias de Bes
PHOTOGRAPHY Joan Guillamat

ZARAGOZA DELICIAS INTERMODAL STATION
DATE 2000-2003
ARQUITECTURA Carlos Ferrater - José Mª Valero with Elena Mateu - Félix Arranz
PHOTOGRAPHY Alejo Bagué

FRONTAURA WINERY
DATE 2006
ARCHITECTS Carlos Ferrater
Xavier Martí
PHOTOGRAPHY Alejo Bagué

MARRIOTT BARCELONA EDITION HOTEL, BARCELONA
DATE 2010-2012
ARCHITECTS Xavier Martí
Carlos Ferrater
PHOTOGRAPHY Joan Guillamat
Alejo Bagué

HOUSING DEVELOPMENT IN PLAÇA DE LESSEPS
DATE 2004-2007
ARCHITECTS Carlos Ferrater
Lucía Ferrater
Xavier Martí
PHOTOGRAPHY Alejo Bagué

VÉRTIX HOUSING
DATE 2003-2007
ARCHITECTS Carlos Ferrater
Xavier Martí
PHOTOGRAPHY Alejo Bagué

AA HOUSE
DATE 2007 - 2009
ARCHITECTS Carlos Ferrater
Xavier Martí
PHOTOGRAPHY Alejo Bagué

BUILDING IN PASSEIG DE GRÀCIA
DATE 2004
ARCHITECTS Carlos Ferrater
with Xavier Martí
and Juan Trias de Bes
PHOTOGRAPHY Alejo Bagué

JUAN CARLOS I HOTEL
DATE 1989 - 1992
ARCHITECTS Carlos Ferrater
with Jose Mª Cartañá

GAS NATURAL BUILDING
DATE 1999
ARQUITECTO Carlos Ferrater

IMQ ZORROTZAURE HOSPITAL
DATE 2010-2012
ARCHITECTS Carlos Ferrater
Alfonso Casares
with Luis Domínguez
and Núria Ayala
STRUCTURAL ENG *Juan Calvo (Pondio)*
PHOTOGRAPHY Joan Guillamat

MUSEUM IN LYON
DATE 2000
ARCHITECTS Carlos Ferrater
with Bruno Dumetier
and Alberto Peñín

BENIDORM SEAFRONT
DATE 2006-2009
ARCHITECTS Carlos Ferrater
Xavier Martí
STRUCTURAL ENG *Juan Calvo (Pondio)*
PHOTOGRAPHY Alejo Bagué
Joan Guillamat

BIBLIOGRAPHIC NOTES

Carlos Ferrater, Borja Ferrater (2006). **Synchronizing Geometry. Landscape, Architecture and Construction.**
Actar ISBN 978-84-96540-34-7
Note 18 p. 8
Note 21 p. 8

Carlos Ferrater (2008).
Casas y Habitantes.
Actar ISBN 978-84-96954-48-9
Note 1 p. 89
Note 10 p. 38
Note 11 p. 41
Note 12 p. Four. Five

OAB. Carlos Ferrater & Partners (2010).
Actar ISBN 978-84-96954-54-0
Note 9 p. 163

Josep Mª Montaner (2012).
Carlos Ferrater. Premio Nacional de Arquitectura 2009. Secretaría General Técnica Centro de Publicaciones. Catálogo de Publicaciones de la Administración General del Estado.
ISBN 978-84-498-0921-7
Note 2 p. 79
Note 3 p. 81
Note 6 p. 75
Note 7 p. 81
Note 8 p. 83
Note 13 p. 54
Note 16 p. 67
Note 17 p. 67
Note 19 p. 61

Note 4. Pedagogical dimensions of Jorge Oteiza's Chalk Laboratory and its application to the Teaching of the Fundamentals of the Architecture Project. http://oa.upm.es/42622/1/INVE_MEM_2015_230524.pdf

Note 14. When he was interviewed in the program "Redes" broadcast on "La 2 de TVE" in February 2007, Punset asked the scientist for an architect who would work with fractal architecture. Mandelbrot made reference to Carlos Ferrater. FRACTAL OBJECTS AND ARCHITECTURE | Final Degree Project ETSAV | Celia Ana Martínez Requena 10

Note 15. Cited by J. Pernas in "Learning by teaching". Ed: 47-61 Editor page 266

Ignacio Paricio Ansuátegui is an architect who is Emeritus Professor at the Universitat Politècnica de Catalunya. He has worked as both an architect and as a researcher and teacher.

The most recent buildings he has designed and built include the Food Research Center (Alicia) near Manresa and the Illa de la Llum skyscraper complex at Diagonal Mar and the Fòrum Geriatric Center, both in Barcelona. The awards he has received include FAD prizes for the restoration of the Llotja de Mar building and Azulete restaurant in Barcelona, the Bank of Spain Building in Girona, a warehouse building in Canovelles, and the town hall at Sant Pere de Ribes. In 1983, he was presented with the National Town Planning Award (with M. Sola Morales); in 1999, he received the Catalan National Award for the Simón Industrial Unit in Olot; and in 2009 he won the Década Award for the Bank of Spain Building in Girona. He has worked with Roberto Terradas, Edgardo Mannino, Oscar Tusquets, and Lluís Clotet.

He led the restoration of landmark buildings such as La Boquería market, the Palau de la Música concert hall, the Convent dels Àngels theater, and the water tank that was converted into a library for Pompeu Fabra University, all in Barcelona. He replaced the dome of Figueres Museum, which was originally built by Dalí and Piñero, for which he received the Construmat Award.

As part of his work researching architecture and construction, he oversaw ITEC's publications studies and IMAT's research on industrialization. He was an adviser to the Spanish Housing Ministry as part of the Council for Sustainability, Innovation, and Regulations.

He has promoted and run five Casa Barcelona events, which were part of Construmat, a construction industry trade show which showcases experimental products seeking to create housing that is better suited to contemporary Spanish society.

He has designed various types of construction components, five of which have been patented: the pieces of the so-called Mediterranean facade, the retractable shutter, the UHPC panel structure, pneumatically watertight sliding windows, and GLS prestressed facade panels.

He has also designed and launched two digital platforms: Filt3rs and Façad3s.

He spent 50 years as a university professor, including at the UPC's School of Architecture for the last 35 years. He has given lectures in many cities in Spain, Europe, and North America. The publication of the trilogy known as "The Construction of Architecture" changed technical teaching systems in many schools of architecture. He has written around 20 books, more than half of which were published by Bisagra, as well as titles like *La piel ligera* (Actar, 2010), *JL Sert, construcción y arquitectura* (Gustavo Gili, 1983), and *La vivienda contemporánea, diseño y tecnología,* written with Xavier Sust (Ed. Itec, 1998).

He was a member of the drafting committees for Spain's Urban Rehabilitation, Regeneration and Renovation Act (Act 8/2013 of June 26) and the Catalan Architecture Act (Act 12/2017 of July 6).

Notes

Notes

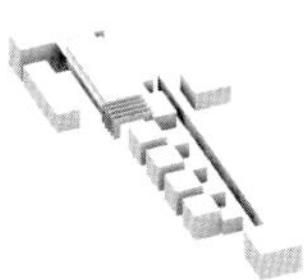

Notes

Notes

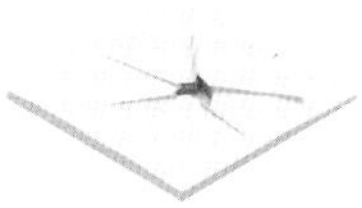

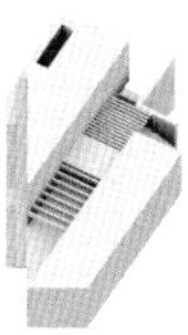

Notes

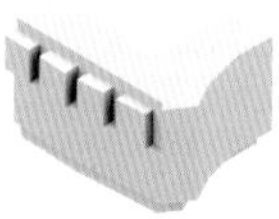

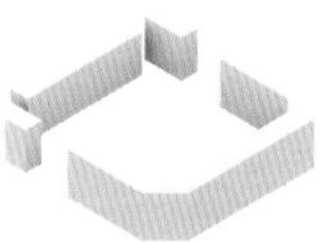

Notes

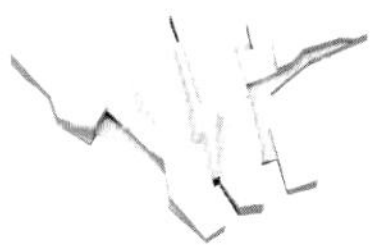

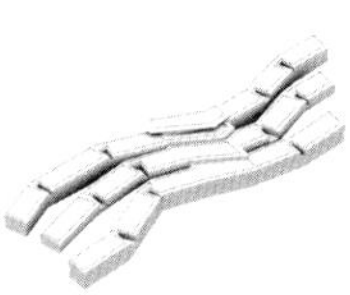

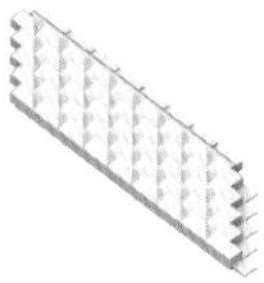

Notes

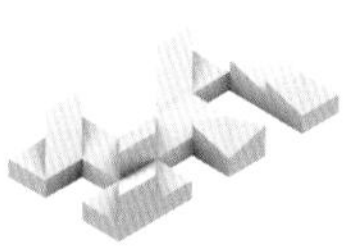

Notes

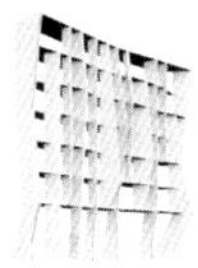

GEOMETRIC TAXONOMY
CARLOS FERRATER & OAB

Published by
Actar Publishers
actar.com

Author
Ignacio Paricio

Distribution
Actar D, Inc.
New York, Barcelona

New York
440 Park Avenue South,
17th Floor
New York, NY 10016, USA
T +1 212 9662207
salesnewyork@actar-d.com

Barcelona
Roca i Batlle 2-4
08023 Barcelona, Spain
T +34 933 282 183
eurosales@actar-d.com

Printed in Barcelona
Two editions: Spanish and English
February 2021

ISBN: 978-1-948765-86-2

Library of Congress Control
Number (PCN): 2021931787